LISA HAMM, PhD

WALKING THROUGH FIRE

OVERCOMING LIFE'S WORST CIRCUMSTANCES

Dr. Lisa
Publishing

© Copyright 2016 Dr. Lisa Hamm. Printed and bound in the United States of America. All rights reserved. No part of this book may be reproduced or transmitted in any form or by any means, electronic or mechanical, including photocopying, recording copying or by an information storage and retrieval system-with the exception of a reviewer who may quote brief passages in a review to be printed in a newspaper or magazine-without written permission from the publisher. For information, contact Dr. Lisa Publishing at drlisaministries.org.

This book includes information from many sources and gathered for many personal experiences. It is published for general reference and is not intended to be a substitute for independent verification by readers when necessary and appropriate. The book is sold with the understanding that neither the author nor publisher is engaged in rendering any legal, psychological or medical advice. The publisher and author disclaim any personal liability, directly or indirectly, for advice or information presented within. Although the author and publisher have prepared this manuscript with utmost care and diligence and have made every effort to ensure the accuracy and completeness of the information contained within, we assume no responsibility for errors, inaccuracies, omissions or inconsistencies.

Hamm, Lisa
Walking Through Fire: Overcoming Life's Worst Circumstances

ISBN-13: 978-1530818839
ISBN-10: 1530818834

SHARE YOUR EXPERIENCE

Friends and Groups are using the companion OVERCOMER'S BOOK GROUP AND PRAYER JOURNAL while reading Walking Through Fire

Suggested book group guidelines and questions INSIDE and room to JOURNAL YOUR JOURNEY!

FOREWORD

Darlene Bishop

Will you make it through? Will the depression and pain ever leave? Does it seem life has lost all meaning, never to be enjoyed again? When you are *WALKING THROUGH FIRE,* you think you may not even make it out alive. If you do, you feel your damage and loss may be too great to overcome.

You did not see it coming. In its element of surprise, it is deceptive, divisive, destructive, and deadly. The realization dawns that some fires are a source of evil. You need strategies to fight, for the fire seeks to steal, kill, and destroy.

Fire increases in intensity when fueled, and it causes you to want to give up. When surrounded by flames, you must know that you are not alone in the experience.

Others have preceded you and overcome more trauma than you can imagine. Yet they survived. Knowing their difficulties and accompanying them through their fire can get you through yours.

As a spiritual mother and mentor to Dr. Lisa Hamm, the author of this book, I was one in the body of Christ who accompanied her through her walk through fire. I helped her navigate the many intense trials she faced by keeping in mind the parable of the potter's wheel that God gave to Jeremiah. We are all vessels of clay, and the hotter the temperature of the fire, the more precious the vessel.

I have known Lisa for more than two decades and now that she is ministering as a Christian communicator, I encouraged her to write this book. Whether you or someone close to you has undergone tremendous loss, suffered from a debilitating illness, endured overwhelming hardship, lacked the resources to defend themselves from enemies, or dealt with terrible consequences for a poor decision, this book is for you!

Read every sentence closely and enjoy the encounters with God in each chapter. They are present because God wants to heal your wounds and deliver you from whatever may be holding you back. If you are still in the fire, continue to walk. Hold this book in your hand with the Word of God and allow the pain and anguish you are feeling to make you cling to Him. You *will* persevere. You *will* overcome. Eventually you will walk out of the fire and you will not smell of smoke.

*****

Darlene Bishop Ministries *(DarleneBishop.org)* is an outreach of Solid Rock Church, in Monroe, Ohio, where Darlene shares pastoral duties with her son, Lawrence Bishop II. Darlene began preaching in 1984 at local women's

meetings and in her home church, but her ministry began to expand nationally in 1998. Darlene Bishop Ministries is now traveling full-time, and she appears regularly on international Christian television programs. This ministry was established to reach the loss, the broken, and the hurting, and to reveal that victory can be obtained every time, if only you BELIEVE.

The compassion Darlene has shown through the various ministries that she has founded and supports, such as the Home for Life and the Brazilian Orphanage. Darlene Bishop Ministries is spreading the Gospel across the nation and around the world.

PREFACE

Allow Walking Through Fire to be a literary treasure you return to often.

-Dr. Lisa

Thank you so much for reading this book and for connecting with Dr. Lisa Ministries. I have written this book for you. I have a deep love of God in my heart for you. I hope this book and the Word of God heals you in every area of your life.

I want to be present with you on your journey, to connect with you at eye level. I am sharing my WALK THROUGH FIRE, for I hope that the Holy Spirit can use it to minister to your life.

My own fire experience will be much more worth it if I know that it helps you. I pray the transparency and vulnerability in the pages in this book encourages you and gives you revelation in areas of need. Even though we have yet to meet, I pray for you right now, that God would put this book in your hands and give you supernatural strength to make you an overcomer.

I sincerely hope this book profoundly impacts you as much as writing it has for me. Each chapter speaks to specific needs and has a completely different purpose of ministering and educating while you are WALKING THROUGH FIRE.

Take your time. If you are not an avid reader, do not let the length of this book intimidate you. Savor each sentence. Allow Walking Through Fire to be a literary treasure you return to often. I wish I had a book like this available to me on my journey so much that I am determined to make it available to you.

For maximum impact, you should read this book with at least one other trusted friend, preferably a person with whom you are able to vent and be completely vulnerable. It is important to be able to share secret hurts and deep thoughts while reading for complete healing of the soul.

This book is also strongly suggested for book groups of 8-11 people. If possible, use the companion to this book, the OVERCOMER'S JOURNAL. The Overcomer's Journal includes suggested book group guidelines and questions. It also has room for recording your prayers and thoughts on your reading journey. It is best that some of the subject matter is processed with other mature Christians. Also, remember to unite in prayer asking the Holy Spirit for revelation, guidance, and healing each time you read this book and in each book group gathering.

If you do not have a friend that will read the book together with you at this time, make sure you stay connected with me online at drlisaministries.org.

At times I may get bogged down in technical, theological explanations and it may seem that I am ignoring human pain and suffering, but eventually you will see me get back on course. This book explores different avenues while I was looking for answers to the many questions in what I now call my *walk through fire*. Over the past several years I have been through so much pain and anguish that at times, due to their depths, I did not want to continue living.

Although I am someone who believes in the goodness of the world, I was extremely naïve about the presence of evil. God's Word provided comfort, guidance, and direction in every way, but in my journey I realized I also needed to understand what was happening to me psychologically and emotionally. I did not recognize myself in that season of grief, loss, and injustice. I became a different person at different stages and intensities of the fire. I needed to understand what was causing me to become so unrecognizable. And I needed to know what to do about it.

I delved into research on the mind and what happens to people who endure deep suffering. I am happy to say I found meaning in the pain I endured and was on my way to healing.

Someone once said God does not waste a hurt. I knew that one day I would write this book. Actually, I began writing it a couple years ago. It started with my experience when I was processed criminally after sitting in a jail cell for a day. I actually thought that day was going to be the worst one I had ever experienced, but I was wrong.

I am likening this book to a walk through fire because I have both figuratively and literally walked through fire. I say *walking through fire* figuratively because of intensity of the heat and pressure of the pain and suffering I endured over several years. I say it literally because one time I actually went to an Anthony Robbins seminar and walked across hot coals of fire at a stage when I thought I could think myself out of the pain.

Can you believe the things we do sometimes?

I am hopeful this book prepares you for success in healing your wounds and using them, or the *ITs in your life*, to give birth to a new vision and purpose.

Join me in this figurative walk through fire especially if you are literally walking through it right now. We are going to overcome. Our walk *through* fire will get us *to* the greatest season of our lives not smelling of smoke.

ABOUT THE AUTHOR

Dr. Lisa Hamm is a multidimensional professional communicator and leader and has a PHD in Educational Leadership. As CEO of Dr. Lisa Ministries, she serves as a Christian speaker, teacher, and coach for

the body of Christ. As a John Maxwell Certified trainer, she serves organizations internationally by providing customized presentations to fit individual needs.

Dr. Lisa is one of America's best pioneers in the field of education. She has contributed workable solutions to the Urban Education Crisis that exists today. Further, she built three different organizations that became highly successful and made a difference in the lives of thousands of youth and educators. She has also authored two books for educator development. As a missionary, Dr. Lisa has experienced great moves of God internationally while serving as an evangelist and teacher.

Dr. Lisa became a born again Christian at age seven at a Billy Graham crusade. She grew up in the small town of Ludlow, Kentucky active in the Southern Baptist Church. In most of her adult life she was active at Solid Rock Church in Monroe, Ohio where she was mentored by Pastor Darlene Bishop. Currently, Dr. Lisa is active at Community Family Church in Independence, Kentucky with Pastor Tommy Bates as her spiritual covering.

Dr. Lisa's desire is to influence and facilitate personal growth globally and profoundly impact lives. It is her hope the truths in God's Word will help us overcome our walk *through* fire to get *to* the greatest season of our lives not smelling of smoke.

DEDICATION

I would like to dedicate *WALKING THROUGH FIRE* to my parents Nelson and Rena Hamm. I am forever mindful and grateful to be blessed with having had them as parents. Even though they have both gone on to be with the Lord, they continue to be my strength and inspiration.

To my mother, Rena Bryant Hamm, thank you for being the best mother anyone could have, and for encouraging me to become my best and not to let anything hold me back.

To my dad, Nelson (Sonny) Hamm, thank you for being an amazing father, for modeling hard work and demonstrating what a real family man should be, helping me to not settle for less than God's best in my personal life.

ACKNOWLEDGEMENTS

To my Lord and Savior, Jesus Christ: Thank You for entrusting me to deliver this literary treasure. I thank God for giving me loving and supportive people in my life such as my best friend Pam and her husband Larry, and spiritual mentors and friends Pastor Tommy Bates and Tara and the wonderful saints at Community Family Church. You have nurtured me and sharpened me as "Iron Sharpens Iron."

I am forever thankful for the mentorship and friendship of Pastor Darlene Bishop who has demonstrated how to come out of the fire not smelling of smoke. She has shown me how God is using women to build the kingdom in these last days. Also to Pastor Lawrence Bishop, who has gone on to be with the Lord, but has forever imprinted his spiritual wisdom on my heart. He was a man of great vision who modeled how to believe God for a dream and bring it forth for His glory.

I appreciate John Maxwell for his mentorship and sharing his expertise in leadership over the last few decades. You have inspired me to touch the hearts of the masses in all environments across the globe.

I also want to thank my family – Rick, Audrea, Steven, Elizabeth, Carmen, and Abbigail Hamm for support in both the best and worst of times. When one member of a family walks through fire at some level the entire family does. Thanks for persevering.

Finally, there can never be a great book without great contributors to the process. Thank you Darlene Bishop, Pamela Carter, Steve Coomer, Carmen Hamm, Cleda Hoskins, Kishore Kumar, Phil Loughnane, Jill Marie, Katina Morrison, O Magazine, Anthony Vannoy, and all of the members of my Bible Scholars class at Community Family Church.

Contents

FOREWORD	iv
PREFACE	viii
ABOUT THE AUTHOR	xiv
DEDICATION	xvi
ACKNOWLEDGEMENTS	xvii
INTRODUCTION	1
ONE	
What is your *IT*?	7
TWO	
Fireproof	32
THREE	
Evil Intentions	66
FOUR	
Destiny Deferred	94

FIVE
> A Hint from Heaven　　　　　　　　113

SIX
> Taunting Letters　　　　　　　　　133

SEVEN
> Bad News from God　　　　　　　140

EIGHT
> Stairway to Fear　　　　　　　　　154

NINE
> Paralyzed　　　　　　　　　　　　184

TEN
> Intellectual Faith　　　　　　　　　204

ELEVEN
> Wise Humility　　　　　　　　　　229

TWELVE
> Spirit-Led Approach　　　　　　　243

THIRTEEN

    Prayer Strategies in the Fire   278

FOURTEEN

    Power in the Process   301

FIFTEEN

    Release Reach Remain   317

SIXTEEN

    Appointment with God   332

SEVENTEEN

    The Invitation   340

STAY CONNECTED!   345

INTRODUCTION

Life has its challenges, to say the least. Anyone who has a pulse has problems - and we all have had seasons when we have walked through fire. Such unbearable challenges are part of life. Too often, it seems that we are coming out of a crisis, in the middle of a crisis, or are headed towards a crisis.

-Dr. Lisa

Many have walked through fire...

The family with insurmountable business, financial, or legal problems that drain all resources...

The woman who was sexually, physically, mentally, and emotionally abused by one she thought she could trust...

The spouse whose has been traded in for a newer model...

The public person under constant scrutiny from gawkers and overzealous critics...

The youth forced to choose which parent to live with because of divorce...

The child left in a dumpster at birth...

Some effects are invisible while others are obvious:

The soldier dismembered in battle...

The woman who has just had a double mastectomy...

The beauty queen with the jealous boyfriend who lit her entire body on fire who must live with irreparable physical, mental, and emotional disfiguration...

Others have experienced unspeakable massive calamity:

The natural catastrophe that wiped out an entire community...

The mother who learned that one son killed the other in a gun accident...

The Holocaust victim who has experienced "never forget" every day of his life...

We question.

We have prayed, worshiped, brought tithes, and been faithful in church. We have been trustworthy and honorable human beings. When trouble suddenly arrives on our doorstep, we are shocked to find that no amount of righteousness has exempted us from this unbearable walk:

She was a good wife, but he still left.

He was a good husband, yet she still cheated.

She was a good mother, but her kids still cursed her.

We have been broken, tried, and tested in confusing ways.

Where did we go wrong? What has happened? We have asked the Lord countless times, "I'm a good person. Why is this happening? My life was not supposed to be like this!"

Life has its challenges, to say the least. Anyone who has a pulse has problems -

and we all have had seasons when we have walked through fire. Such unbearable challenges are part of life. Too often, it seems that we are coming out of a crisis, in the middle of a crisis, or are headed towards a crisis.

Still, there is no need to face these challenges alone. If we allow them and work through them, the fire walk can bring goodness to our lives – like when God told Jeremiah to go to the Potter's House. There, God began to demonstrate His promise to take all our brokenness and make it strong and sturdy. Make it useful. Make it amazing.

I want to assure you that you will get through your fire and that you are not facing it without help. God will use this challenge to make your life greater than you could ever imagine.

Though the fire may at times be intense, as God has promised through the prophet Isaiah: "Do not be afraid. For I have bought you and made you free. I have called you by name. You are Mine! When you pass through the waters, I will be with you. When you pass through the rivers, they will not flow over you. When you walk through the fire, you will not be burned. The fire will not destroy you" (Isaiah 43:1-2 NLV). That is God's promise. The fire will not destroy us. Not only will we survive, but God *will* use our walk through fire for good. The affirmation that hangs just above the door to my garage reminds me: "I HAVE SURVIVED. NOW I WILL THRIVE." Dear reader, know that you are not alone right now. There are many people praying for you before this book was ever placed in your hands. Ecclesiastes 4:9-10 says, "Two *are* better than one, Because they have a good reward for their labor. ¹⁰ For if they fall, one will lift up his companion. But woe to him *who is* alone when he falls, For *he has* no one to help him up." (NKJV) Take my hand. Together we will overcome our walk *through* the fire to get *to* the greatest season of our lives not smelling of smoke. Double for our trouble!

Let us repeat this declaration as we stand in agreement:

> I will get through this because God is with me.
>
> My walk through the fire may be painful,
>
> And it may be long,
>
> But with God's help I will overcome.
>
> In the meantime, I will be wise and hopeful because
>
> God will use IT for good.

Yes, God will use the test, trial, tribulation, or injustice on your life for good. Taking the focus off of your pain and suffering and putting it onto the goodness of God can seem insurmountable. Walking in wisdom and maintaining hope may feel impossible. Yet through the encounters in each chapter, please look for God. Expect to see Him and have hope in Him.

ONE

What is your *IT*?

While walking through fire, I had to remind myself of the times God protected me, delivered me from harm, and brought me prosperity, yet I must admit that those times became faint, especially in the most intense moments.

– Dr. Lisa

What is your *IT*?

No matter who we are, how old or young, there is always at least one point in our lives when *IT* happens – that thing in life that we cannot seem to escape, fix, or solve. Just when we think we may have figured out a little piece of *IT*, how we might be able to handle *IT*, manage *IT*, work around *IT*, or get out ahead of *IT*, *IT* always seems to end up beating us and leads to confusion; feelings of helplessness;

powerlessness; worry, anxiety, and fear as well as depression and despair.

We try – to the point of exhaustion. We pray. We plead. We worry. We plan, calculate, and analyze. We try to approach *IT* from different angles. Sometimes we approach *IT* in an assertive manner. And when that does not work, we become submissive. We are gentle, but when that does not yield results, we get firm. We admit we were wrong and refuse to gloat when we were right. We exhaust every option we find.

We seriously start to wonder how God can allow *IT* and if He is ever going to help us.

We know He can help us... By faith... Because of what God's word says, we know He *can*, yet we begin to wonder if He *will*.

That is really the question. We know God can do whatever He wants to do, but will He choose to do so: *That* is what terrifies us.

We become disgusted with all the church rhetoric, not because we do not want to believe the promises in the word of God, but deep down our souls pulse with doubt and unease.

Why have our circumstances not changed? Why has this life issue, this dilemma we are facing, not gone away? And worse, why has it gotten yet more intense? We begin to question everything about God, perhaps even His existence or His competence to aid us. Can He help us with *IT*? Will He help us with *IT*?

What is *IT*, that which put you on your walk through fire? It's okay. Be honest. Name *IT*.

Trust me – it is better to get *IT* out in the open. To extinguish the intensity of the flames while we walk through this fire, we must be honest and deal in the real.

Let us meet at eye level now. If it makes it easier, I will go first.

In my *IT*, or rather my series of *IT*s, if you will, I landed in the middle of a flaming inferno. A fiery furnace so intense I could neither see nor breathe. My sole goal was to get out alive as soon as I could, but I could not. I was stuck. I was alone. Standing still did not help. I was desperately trying to move in all directions, hoping to find the exit, but I did not. My panic rose when I realized my powerlessness. All my resources had been used up, and I became angry, desperate, deeply depressed, and in a state of despair to the point that I prayed my life would end.

This *IT*, this walk through fire, completely caught me off guard, though that was probably a good thing because had I known the intensity of the fire and the duration of the fire, I do not know if I would have made it. Still, my experiences carved out such a deep crevice that doubt took a foothold in my soul. This level of doubt manifested many different spiritual, emotional, mental, and physical conditions designed to steal, kill, and ultimately destroy. God loves us far too much to keep us from confronting these *ITs*. If we do not turn to face them, we might never come face-to-face with Him.

*****

So, what are my *ITs*?

I was raised in Ludlow, Kentucky, a small, close-knit town that winds alongside the Ohio River. The town was filled with ongoing family activities in the park, football stadium, athletic club, school, churches, and local stores with frequent magical sounds of trains passing by in the background. Everything my family did was in this little town. Both of my parents worked in the town. My brother and I went to school in the town. My dad also went to school there, having grown up in the town. We played sports at the athletic club in the town, and we went to church in the town. There was rarely much we needed outside of it and life was good.

Since the time I was thirteen years old, my life consisted of working, going to school, playing sports, and going to church. As soon as I got out of high school, I was able to go to college because I received a grant for low income families. But I still lived at home. I was scared to leave my mom because my mother had been diagnosed with a debilitating illness known as scleroderma. This disease causes hardening of all of the tissue in the body, including the organs and the skin. I can remember that Mom would experience cycles in which her hands and feet would have hundreds of splits that looked like deep paper cuts. I would help by applying a special medical cream, and during these cycles she always wore gloves and socks. Many people with scleroderma have the same kinds of splits in their skin. (The next time you have a paper cut or a split in your skin and notice the pain, say a prayer for the people with this disease.) This disease caused the most damage to my mom's lungs, which is what led to her death. Yet, I am so thankful that this disease did not affect her brain. We were able to maintain a close relationship all through the time of this illness because her brain remained sound, even though some people with scleroderma do not escape brain tissue deterioration.

My mother was my best friend and my biggest champion in life. She sacrificed everything for my brother and me. The only time we were apart was in the summer months in college when I was a foreign missionary in Brazil. Although Mom never complained of her sickness, over time it was clear that her body was wearing out, partly from the disease itself and partly from the medication and ineffective treatments. I was able to become a teacher, but my mother encouraged me to get an advanced degree. She was determined to live long enough to see me finish my master's degree. She did, but she died two weeks after I graduated. I remember seeing her asleep in the stands at the ceremony. I knew that was not a good sign because my mother was always active. It is terrifying to watch a loved one deteriorate and slip away. It is a powerless feeling.

After my mother's death I continued teaching in a large urban school district in

Ohio just across the river from Kentucky where I grew up. I loved my students and had great success as a teacher, but I endured several years of harassment from a male principal who supervised me. Many times I went to work in fear of what might happen but I was rescued from the situation several years later. I had been given a promotion in the district to assistant principal. Although this was great leadership experience, something about this role did not feel right with me. I knew I had a purpose to do something else. In my second year as assistant principal at one of the toughest schools in the city, I was given divine direction to start a school. (I will give you more details on this later.)

It was grueling but what started as swamp land in the ghetto became a great success. In fact, it became one of the top charter schools in the state of Ohio. The school was thriving and had a very high rating with 1000 students that were high poverty but also high achieving. It was a miracle. The school was succeeding so much that I expanded and opened up a second school and finally a preschool.

I had committed myself so much to the mission God had given me in the inner city that I never had time for a personal life, so I never found the man of my dreams, a life partner. I decided to start a family even though I was single, and I began the adoption process through the foster care system. I was only going to adopt one child, but I was asked to take a family of three so that the children would not be separated. On a beautiful April day I became the mother of two girls and a boy (ages 3, 5, and 6 at the time), but I had to wait 10 months to begin the adoption process. I fell completely in love with my three children and they felt the same. They had never been in a stable environment and had often been severely neglected. Still, nearly a year later, in a meeting I thought was going to be an adoption planning meeting did not turn out that way. Instead I was informed that I was not going to be able to adopt my children, and that they were going to be reunited with their biological father that afternoon. It was 3:00 p.m. on a Monday and I had to take my children, now ages 4, 5, and 7, right after school, from the home they knew and the mother they loved to live in a strange home. Within three hours, my children were gone and with the exception of a few visits afterwards, I never saw them again. The social worker on the case felt maintaining a relationship would be too confusing for the children because they called me "mommy" and had come to know me as such. We were permitted to talk on the phone for a few weeks. I can remember my four year old daughter crying and saying, "Mommy, please come and get me and tell my daddy that I don't live here! Tell him I live with you!" I was at least grateful that I was able to pack up all of their things and ensure that my children got them. My youngest would not have been able to function without her Dora doll for sure. When I got them they had nothing but worn out faded clothes that were too small. I wanted them to at least be able to maintain some normalcy.

This loss was unbearable. But even more losses were coming.

One month after I lost my children, the school I started had become a great success. But in the thirteenth year of operation we began to have horrendous legal issues. There had always been a huge political battle from one entity or another for Charter Schools in Ohio because the education reform movement had many enemies. But this time was different. There was a full-fledged witch hunt launched against me personally. It all started with a disgruntled employee making a false anonymous fraud tip. A criminal investigation was launched from the state auditor's office of Ohio against the school, which resulted in criminal charges against the school leadership, and me specifically, as CEO. (I will give more details about this issue later.)

At the same time the legal battles persisted, my dad was diagnosed with cancer. He had been living with me for the last ten years, and had been very healthy. The treatments did work for the first couple years. Initially the treatments were successful and he was able to stop the chemotherapy for over a year, but the cancer cells were aggressive and the fight had to start all over again right during the time I was fighting this horrendous legal battle right (after I lost my children.)

Dad would have the chemotherapy drugs hooked up to his veins at Veteran's Hospital, and I would be sitting in the chair next to him typing on my laptop trying to sift through all of the ridiculous false accusations and 12,000 pages of auditor work pages, policies, and anything else I could find to defend myself against criminal charges. (More on this later also.)

My dad was in his late 70s and had a job at the school as a member of the building team (facilities and administrative building support) and he made only $250.00 per week. When he had retired from his previous job at a company in our town he had come to work at the school. Dad was very dependable. We could count on him to arrive early in the morning and get the building open and ready for the day. Until dad, this had been a major issue. He had become a father figure for everyone. All of the adults called him "Dad" and the children called him "Pawpaw." He would stand at the entrance of the school every morning welcoming the children and reminding them to go to the cafeteria to eat breakfast. He arrived every morning before 5:00 a.m. to ensure all the teacher's classrooms were unlocked for them, the school animals were tended, and the laundry for swim classes and athletics were ready for the day. Most importantly, he had a contagious laugh and carried a very pleasant spirit throughout the school, which played a big part in the warm inviting family atmosphere obvious to everyone.

Experts say it is important for cancer patients to stay active. Continuing to work is very good if they can still work because such engagement increases recovery rates; and that stress should be minimized. However, the destruction that occurred at the school made this impossible. My precious loving father was treated very badly. He was reporting to work for nearly two weeks and working but his contract had been terminated without him being informed. Guess how we found out?

One day after work, dad had arrived home to find I was not there. I was in a legal office preparing for trial. Dad just had chemotherapy treatments the week before so he was very weak, but he continued to report to work because he did not want any issues to arise from his absence. He noticed something was medically wrong but he could not reach anyone in the family because he could not use his cell phone. It turned out he was having heart complications from the chemotherapy he had been taking.

Why couldn't he reach our family in the emergency? The school had cut his cell phone off unbeknownst to him that day which was apparently the method that was chosen to let him know he was no longer an employee. He did not have any of the family cell numbers memorized to call us from the home landline. With cell phones being a new phenomenon to him, and the fact that he had a very limited skill set when it came to using any form of technology, (as is the case with many older people who did not grow up with technology), he had no idea the school simply cut his cell phone off. He just thought he was not working it properly. He drove himself to the hospital and someone from the hospital was able to contact me as the emergency contact from their system. Have you ever received a phone call like that?

I arrived at the hospital as soon as I could along with my sister-in-law, Audrea, and while we were there with him, dad had a heart attack. He was surrounded by medical personnel so he received the help needed to recover but he was not able to receive any more treatments for the cancer. The chemotherapy was too hard on other parts of his body. So this meant that dad knew the cancer would rapidly spread. We were terrified but tried not to show it.

While he was recovering from a heart attack in the hospital, one of his friends that worked with him visited and informed us that his contract had not been renewed and that his cell phone had been cut off that day. I examined his cell phone and felt rage because of the way this was handled. If I had known I would have made sure he had another way to contact me. The people my dad had loved and supported for more than a decade who had referred to him as "dad" or "pops", had treated him with such disregard. They had let him walk around the school building continuing to work without telling him that his contract was terminated. He worked at least two weeks and did not get any pay and most importantly, he did not receive kindness and consideration in any form. Our hearts were broken.

As the weeks passed all of his friends at work had abandoned him in his time of need with the exception of one other elderly gentleman. This part affected me more than it did him. With the loss of his beloved wife, my mother, two decades prior, he only had our family and his friends. And now he did not have his friends. At least not the friends he spent every day with at work.

Dad would cry as he watched the accusations against me coming across the television news stations. This part affected him much more than it did me. It is hard to see a strong man cry. I regretted even starting that school so much when I saw the tears streaming down my father's face. In the late spring of that year, dad died from the cancer, and I am certain its progression was largely due to the stress my family was under because of the legal crisis.

While dad had cancer, Rita, a close childhood friend who grew up with me, had it as well. She passed away in March and dad passed away just two months later. (More on Rita later.)

Through a series of events after four years, the state auditors of Ohio had successfully completed a witch hunt, a campaign of destruction. I was the prime target. I was falsely accused of criminal activity, my reputation and my Christian witness was ruined in the community. I was ostracized from everyone in my profession. I was drained of my resources. And my life work and freedom were stolen.

If you are not an animal lover please excuse this next paragraph, but for those who are, I think you will relate to this perfectly.

Through this trauma what brought me the most peace seemed to be the unconditional love I received from my pets, Max and Shiloh, both Yorkshire Terriers. Pets can give us the experience of unconditional love and support that often times we cannot get from people. Max, or Maxwell Nelson Hamm formerly, was perfect. He was named after my mentor, John Maxwell, and his middle name was after my dad. He was so perfect that everyone who met Max became an instant dog lover whether they had been previously or not and they dreamed of having a dog like Max. Many ended up getting a yorkie in attempts to have a dog like Max, but he was special. I say *was* because shortly after I was home after having been incarcerated (which was terribly traumatic having to leave them especially after my dad had also just passed away), my dog Max passed away from heart failure. I had taken him to the veterinarian to schedule a teeth cleaning and I was told he had a heart murmur and the vet prescribed a heart murmur pill. Immediately after taking the pill Max began to convulse. I rushed him to the vet and he died 30 minutes after taking the pill. Three hours later my friends were helping me cover Max with a blanket, put him in a decorative box, and bury him in the back yard under a pine tree.

So, to recap, my *IT* or my series of *IT*s are...

When I decided to adopt three children and after raising them as my own for one year, the process did not go through and they were taken away. While my father and a close friend were both facing different types of cancer at the same time, I was in the midst of a terrible legal battle with opponents who had limitless power and resources. My opposition created a highly successful false narrative that rendered me powerless. Over a period of four years, *IT* destroyed my reputation, ruined my relationships, stole my legacy, robbed me of my life savings, and ended my life work. In its midst, two of the people I loved the most died months apart and I lost my beloved Max.

Whew! There *IT* is, or rather, my series of *IT*s.

To avoid a constant repetition of the details, I gave *IT* a name – my *walk through fire*.

There are common experiences we all share with our *IT*s, our walk through fire. We may notice our belief systems are challenged. We might even question the power of God. For most of my life, I have never had much trouble believing in God's power. While walking through fire, I had to remind myself of the times God protected me, delivered me from harm, and brought me prosperity, yet I must admit that those times became faint, especially in the most intense moments. When we are in the fire, we wonder when it is ever going to end, when we will ever get relief, when God will save us, or why God does not help us.

For long periods, I battled such thoughts. Throughout my walk through fire, I stayed faithful in church, consistent in Bible study, and committed to prayer, but at times I became engulfed in anger and frustration because *IT* was not only not changing, but rather getting worse. I was not getting the miracle or the victory that I had expected. I was not able to conquer the giant I thought I would vanquish with the hand of God by my side.

Often, I would listen to people's testimonies about how God made them victorious over a situation and find myself furious. Why? Because it seemed for me, there was no evidence of God's help in sight. I knew that I was not experiencing victory, and I felt that I did not deserve what was happening to me. I became so angry I told God He was lazy, because he was not helping me overcome my adversaries while I was trying to serve Him.

There was a period of time that I could not even pray. I tried but I could not. My loss of faith terrified me. I felt powerless and unable to express myself to God. I was unable to call on Him as I had in the past, but I simply would call out, "God help me, please."

Somehow, I know we can all relate.

While I was walking through fire, I had no sense of security, stability, or balance. I felt insufficient, incapable, and powerless. I had become paralyzed from fear and confusion.

Regardless of feelings or thoughts or lack of results, still I continued to seek.

*****

In the 1989 movie, *Dead Poets Society*, maverick English teacher John Keating inspires a class of male students to seize the day. Played by Robin Williams, Keating tells them to follow their dreams as unique individuals of value. The most memorable moment from this film was the day when Professor Keating first meets his students. He does what is known by educators as the instructional "anticipatory set," the hook to get the students' attention and to create an interesting and memorable lesson.

Professor Keating intrigues the students by having them gaze deeply into old photographs of academic legends. He prompts the young men to savor the wisdom of the literary giants, yet emphasizes that they were people just like them. Here is the hook for us. Keating challenged his students to think of each author in a different way: "They're not that different from you, are they? Same haircuts, full of hormones, just like you. Invincible, just like you feel. The world is their oyster. They believe they're destined for great things. Just like many of you, their eyes are full of hope. Did they wait until it was too late to make their lives even one iota of what they were capable? Because you see gentlemen, these boys are now fertilizing daffodils. But if you listen real close, you can hear them whisper their legacy to you. Go on, lean in. Listen, you hear it? – 'Carpe' — hear it? – 'Carpe. Carpe diem!' Seize the day boys! Make your lives extraordinary."

As we walk through fire, realize the encounters we have on our journey are not much different from others who have gone before us. Maybe the hairstyles have changed, but they are still just like us. They once felt invincible, with the world as their oyster, full of hope, destined for great things, just like us, and then came the fire.

But the fire did not destroy them.

They survived.

Some thrived.

And when they got through the fire, they realized they were entering the greatest season of their lives and they did not smell of smoke.

We will overcome.

As we close each chapter, let us recite the Overcomer's Creed:

I will get through this because God is with me.

My walk through fire may be painful,

And it may be long,

But with God's help I will overcome.

In the meantime, I will be wise and hopeful because

God will use *IT* for good.

TWO

Fireproof

It is terrible when people against us have the power and resources to decide our fate, and to determine the temperature in which we must face it.

- Dr. Lisa

My *IT* came at an unexpected time in a very unexpected way. Before I tell you how, I should first give you some background.

As a young woman, I was a youth minister and athletic coach. I always knew I wanted to work with kids, so in college, I began studying to be an elementary school teacher. When I was studying, over the summer, I was called into the mission field and served in Brazil as an English Teacher and an Evangelist. Later, I became a builder of homes for Habitat for Humanity in Mexico. It was exciting to know I was accomplishing something meaningful for

God with my life. I wanted to know, more than anything, that I was in the center of God's will and that I was being prepared for great work in His kingdom. These experiences were huge spiritual markers in my life and set me on a firm path of always seeking God's will where I could best serve Him, building up the Kingdom of God.

After college, I immediately became a teacher in the inner city and after some years of teaching, I became an assistant principal. It always seemed like God was putting me in challenging, seemingly impossible work situations, but that was always exciting to me. I was on the track to be principal in this large urban district, when I received a prophetic dream followed with a visitation from the demonic, which changed the trajectory of my life.

One particular night, I dreamed I was on a school tour with a group of people. We were walking through a school building observing, and I particularly noticed the warm, inviting atmosphere and how happy the children were in this school. In this dream, I knew I was supposed to know where I was, but felt too embarrassed to ask. I decided to wait until the school tour was over to look on the school marquee or outside on the building to find out the name of the school. This place was nothing short of miraculous and I just remember all of the happy children. And they were all African-American. Finally, the point came when I was able to look outside to see the name of the school on the building. Rena Bryant Hamm, my mother's name, was on the front of the building. As soon as I saw it, the sign must have shocked me awake because I realized this was my school. There is nobody in the world except for me who would have named a school after my mother.

My mother died just before I got my promotion from fourth grade teacher to assistant principal. As I shared in my series of *ITs*, she was fighting a debilitating illness, but was determined to live until I finished my Master's degree. Mom was only able to go to school through the eighth grade because she had to take care of all of her other siblings and the family farm. She constantly told me if I got my education, I would not have to endure the hardship she had in her life. She and my dad sacrificed everything they could so my brother and I could have a better life and receive the best education possible. Our parents also gave us a strong work ethic, and since the age of 13, I always had a job and went to school simultaneously. (Still, my mother was wrong about the hardship. Education does not prevent it. Nothing does.)

Now back to my dream about a school building with my mother's name on it. When I opened my eyes, I could not move my body one inch, it was like I was paralyzed, and I heard very clearly in my spirit that I was going to start a school. Once I heard this I was suddenly able to move. I sat up and said, "Lord, How am I going to do this?" I turned on the television and immediately Jesse Duplantis popped on the screen saying, "Don't ask God how you're going to do something. When He tells you to do something, He'll let you know when He needs you to know!" Or something to that effect.

Immediately after Jesse said that, the television went off. A few moments later, a very dark figure came into the room. It looked exactly like the character from the movie based on Charles Dicken's *Christmas Carol*, the ghost of Christmas past. The dark figure with a black hooded robe had no face. It pointed its very long skeletal finger directly at me. As I sat up in my bed the dark figure said, "If you do that I will kill you!"

I do not know how anyone else would have reacted, but for me I immediately needed to release my bladder. Yet, I was too terrified to move. I told the demonic presence to leave; I started simply, saying the name of Jesus over and over again. Immediately the presence turned and left the room. Thank goodness I have not seen it since. However, one day I was watching an interview where a female evangelist described this very same visitor who came to her on three separate occasions and she described it as the spirit of death.

I hope I'm not freaking anyone out too much, but this really happened.

*****

The very next day I had breakfast with someone who gave me a brochure. She told me she felt directed by God to give it to me. Guess what it was? Information on how to start something called a charter school. From the brochure I could see this was a privately run public entity that could begin grassroots, from the ground up. I knew God was all over this because just the night before I had a very clear supernatural encounter ordering my steps to develop the school. So I followed the leading of the Holy Spirit.

From that moment on, I began taking the necessary steps just like Noah building the ark. God gave me directions to start an inner-city charter school. Still, I did not name it after my mother. It seemed the reason my mother's name was in the dream was so the vision would be clear to me. What was overwhelmingly clear was the loving and warm environment that was to be created for children in a very high challenged area. A place where there are very few opportunities for kids to do much in life outside of whatever is in their neighborhood.

The inner city was known to be a difficult place for a small town white girl from Kentucky, but I believed it the setting for my calling. Although I had no children of my own, I loved my students as if they were mine. I put my heart and soul into teaching and the students in my classrooms thrived. After I finished college I still wanted to learn as much as possible, for I wanted my students to have the best. With encouragement from my loved ones, I continued to get advanced degrees, earned National Board Certification, and practically lived at the staff development center for the district. It seemed God consistently put me in each position to develop me and then prompted me to take on bigger challenges, especially in the areas of leadership. So my elementary teaching position soon led to an assistant principal role. Then, by what was divine inspiration, I started a school in the inner city and committed myself fully to the work by stepping out on faith. After about a year, and thousands and thousands of dollars of my own money, the school was ready to open on September 7, 1999.

*****

This school was amazing, but not at first. It took an immense amount of blood, sweat, and tears to develop what became a dream fulfilled and a life work, my personal mission from God that expanded to others who embraced it as their mission too. Since the school started, thousands of children have been able to receive an excellent education while being nurtured through their very impressionable years, surrounded by love while growing up in a tough environment.

In this very dangerous area flooded with crime and deep issues surrounding poverty, limited education, and work opportunities, 81% of the students were dropping out of school, and very few went on to higher education. I committed myself to develop the college preparatory program I believe God led me to create and lead, a program that became one of the top ones in the state. It was as good, if not better, than any private school around (and I say this because in this area private schools have the best reputation for providing the best education), only it was a public charter school with 98% high poverty African American students. The college preparatory school exposed the students to every great opportunity available. We worked to provide the best quality academics, arts, and athletics and focused on providing opportunities to allow students to enjoy being children in a society that causes them to grow up way too quickly. We had 1000 students preschool through twelfth grade with physical education, dance, art, music, science lab, computer lab, and swimming. Yes, swimming. We partnered with the YMCA to build an addition on the back of the elementary school building, so we had a swimming pool with hired life guards for weekly swim lessons as a special class every week. We also had in-house theatre groups come at least monthly, and we participated in as many city cultural events as we could.

Why is all of this so special? Because this was unheard of in public schools, and if parents could not pay for a private education, then the likelihood of a child receiving a quality education was low. Although the students were high poverty, they were also high achieving. Even more importantly, they were educated about purpose and how to pursue it. The result was remarkable. God was doing miracles every day and I loved it. I loved the students and I loved the staff.

It was very hard to keep good teachers and leaders because of the challenges in urban education and being a single start up school. Typically, people start out in the inner city because they cannot find another job and then move on after they have gotten some experience and have been trained. For several years, staff members would take what was poured into them to make them successful, and then they would move on to another job, usually in the suburbs, leaving us to start all over again with an unseasoned staff member. In some ways one cannot fault people who do this because it is very difficult to work under certain types of challenging conditions long term.

In urban education, teachers constantly problem solve issues of having children in the classroom several years behind grade level, many disinterested in learning. They have multiple learning disabilities, behavioral issues, emotional and social issues, and little to no family support. In other words, it is all on the teacher to address all of their needs.

It was especially hard in the early years when I was just developing the school. Those teachers not only had to prepare all of the lessons and teach several subjects in very inadequate facilities with limited resources, but initially, they also had to clean their own classrooms and do whatever other tasks were necessary. Starting the school put me in a boat load of debt for several years. There were issues across the board with facilities, transportation, discipline, staff, and parents, and our resources were very slim. Regardless of the enormous challenges, I knew it was meant to be, so I committed myself fully to it. It was my heart. As a line in the movie Freedom Writers states, "I was blessed with a burden."

To develop the school into a success, I knew the most important part was going to be the leadership and the staff. To attract quality teachers and keep them, school policies were developed to add value to everyone. We wanted to create strong staff development programming and to create a family atmosphere among students and staff. These developments changed the school culture better than I could ever have imagined. The school went from a low performing, chaotic environment to a high performing close-knit family environment.

On a regular basis, we had team building events such as laser tag, sporting events, arts events, and plenty of opportunities to break bread together. It was critical to spend time building relationships while providing opportunities for students and staff. Most staff members had not experienced much of life outside of television, movies, malls, bars, or whatever was on the blocks of their neighborhoods. It was critical for the school to create strategies to cast and navigate the vision, to break the cycles of dysfunction, and to change the landscape of the lives of every person.

It took many years but most people captured a vision for greatness that was constantly cast, and the result for the organization was again a very high performing, tight-knit family oriented school culture. During school programs in urban areas people typically do not see much parental involvement, but this was not the case with this school. This school was standing room only at all events, and the absentee fathers most seen in the

African American community were present right alongside of all other family members.

The school reputation became so great; we began having visitors from various places to see what we were doing and how we were doing it. The school was succeeding in all areas. The students were thriving. All of the accomplishments were praised by everyone, but when the fire came, everyone scattered and I was left to stand alone. I was thrown into the fiery furnace with nobody beside me.

*****

Now here's the *IT*, I referred to in my series of *IT*s, I promised I would share more that came at an unexpected time in a very unexpected way.

The school was investigated for accusations of misspending funds deemed by the state auditors as "not proper public purpose." This accusation caused the most unimaginable intense legal battle over a period of several years. It was truly a witch hunt that resulted in a criminal conviction against me. I never really understood what the term *witch hunt* fully meant until I personally experienced it. Basically, a witch hunt is a campaign formed against a person, usually by people in power, because of unpopular or unorthodox views.

Most people in the business world understand very much how important it is to engage in practices that build a positive work culture and develop employees, but I soon came to realize these views were in the minority and considered criminal acts by the state auditors. The school had operated as much as possible in ways to show appreciation to employees and placed a high value on professional development and team building from day one. Everyone was in agreement with the practices and participated in them including school legal counsel, sponsor, board members, and everyone involved in the school. However, in the end, I became an isolated target and all other school personnel and board members were pressured to cooperate in the efforts auditors made to have me prosecuted.

My dream, the God given mission given to me through divine inspiration, was now stolen from me and being dismantled. What had been an organization led by the Holy Spirit became a typical governmental institution reflected on every other corner of the state. The unique God inspired educational environment was under siege and taken captive. It was being forced back into a traditional school like all other schools operated by the government. This change was accomplished by removing me from the school, charging me criminally, and then taking control of everyone and everything in it, just as in Babylon.

Nobody stood up against the false narrative long term, even though they knew the truth. What was more shocking, a few people became even worse than the original accusers. Some even used my hard work and vision as an opportunity to benefit themselves.

The people working for the state auditor's campaign completely manipulated everyone, twisted every detail to create lies, and broadcasted it throughout the airwaves. The goal was to alienate all of my supporters, and they did eventually. When people hear lies long enough they start to believe them, especially when people who work closely with you for many years go along with the lies.

Most of us can relate to a betrayal of close associates in which not only do they betray us, but they pull the entire rug out from under us. People like this would steal the houses out from under their own mothers. It was most disheartening when I came to realize some of the key people I loved and nurtured for many years took part in the pillaging and justified themselves in doing it.

How many mentors have such experiences with their mentees?

Think about the pastor developing the young aspiring minister, his associate pastor, his mentee, the person he has spent months or maybe years befriending and breaking bread with, eventually discovers the people in groups he is holding in the church basement are now leaving the church, and going with the associate pastor to start a new church.

Think about the business man training the protégé to take on new challenges who later finds out he is out of a job and the new protégé is the new CEO. Scenarios like this happen every day, but what do we do if we are on the losing end?

In my case, after there was a successful takeover of everything I built, the people I loved as my own family took the best of everything I had, even books I know they will never read, and pillaged them. One particular assistant principal tried to even keep my doctoral cap and gown for herself, even though she had not formally earned a degree. She was planning to wear that with pride. So many were like vultures moving in on the fresh kill.

The board president quickly moved in my office and illegally ran the school himself for many months until someone finally caught on to it. He began using the staff and school resources for his own interest like he was personally the CEO. Nobody would stop him because they were too afraid. They feared if they said or did anything to stand up they would be next on the termination list. Every person they viewed in support of me was terminated.

Even though for some reason they were resistant to returning my personal items that remained at the school, some staff members saw the injustice of it all and attempted to return occasional items to me. In fact, they were able to smuggle Romeo, my exotic bird, back home to me that I had at the school for the enjoyment of the students since the first day of school back in 1999.

To let you know a little more about the school environment, I felt the animals were important because most kids in urban areas do not have exposure to animals. The kids were always captivated by all of them. We had birds, snakes, frogs, fish, rabbits and other reptiles. Sometimes they were a nuisance because of the occasional snake or frog that got out of the cage, or the reproduction of animals that we didn't think could reproduce. It was all worth it for the kids. But I knew if I was not there to oversee the care of any of the animals they all would die. Especially given that my dad was the primary person that cared for them.

*****

During the legal crisis most people said nothing and just simply bowed. The team oriented environment, the warm, inviting, loving school culture, had been completely broken down over a period of years and the mentality became all about self preservation, an everyman for himself mindset.

There were not three men in the fire. There was only one woman – me. When I was thrown into the fire, I was shell shocked and naïve. I received a personal, intense, and very costly education in what attorney Jay Sekulow refers to in our nation as the threat from regulatory agencies; the unrecognized fourth branch of government, the most dangerous branch.

Having a great love for my country and as an entrepreneur, I always believed anything was possible if I worked hard enough to achieve it and build it. After my experience I am not so sure.

It seems the government power is expanding by creating crises and problems that really do not exist. It is almost like the state and federal agencies fabricate issues and then trick the public into thinking bigger government is needed to resolve problems that do not exist. And personally I have very extensive experience with bureaucrats forming opinions about something and then using the systems in place against the very individuals the systems were designed to protect.

The governmental agency bureaucracy imposes thousands of new laws every year without a single vote, violating the rights of Americans without accountability—

persecuting various citizens, and damaging our economy with job-killing destructive rules, as stated by Sekulow. In *Undemocratic: How Unelected, Unaccountable Bureaucrats are Stealing Your Liberty and Freedom,* Sekulow argues "Americans are bullied by the very institutions established to protect their right to life, liberty, and the pursuit of happiness. Our nation's bureaucrats are on an undemocratic power trip. It is illegal abuse." So true! Upon discovery of Sekulow's research, I discovered numerous citizens have shared my walk through fire experiences. Some like me betrayed by state, and some betrayed by country. Betrayals like this make it difficult to maintain a servant's heart in the land of the "so-called" free.

*****

Dr. David Jeremiah, Senior Pastor of Shadow Mountain Community Church, taught a sermon series from his book *Agents of the Apocalypse.* In this series he describes in the current day as an age where so many seem to be bowing down and giving into a culture of ungodliness, Christians should be willing to stand up for God, for biblical principles, and for other people who take this stand. This problem is hardly unique to the times in which we live. From the beginning of time, God has called on his people to stand up for truth and righteousness and not bend to cultural pressure.

We can witness the strength and courage of three Hebrew young men in a fiery encounter, as Dr. Jeremiah describes. The faith of the three men had initially elevated them to a place of prominence in Babylon. These exiles were respected, admired, and revered. They lived for God even in an unfamiliar land – a strange and godless culture ridden with sorcery, witchcraft, and carnality.

The three courageous Hebrews stood and stood again, and then another stood with them. There was a fourth man in the fire. When it was all said and done, in standing for God they changed the world around them.

Who were these three fireproof men who took a stand and would not bend a knee to a false God?

Scholars believe there was a 20-year gap between the second and third chapters of Daniel, and during this time something had drastically changed in the heart of King Nebuchadnezzar. At first, the king makes a glorious tribute to Daniel and to Daniel's God, and he elevated their status in the kingdom. But something changed and there was a shift in the atmosphere.

How often have these invisible shifts happened in our own lives?

Daniel was no longer elevated in the King's mind. The King had decided to compel his subjects to worship a common idol – a massive 90 foot tall grotesque self-image made of gold to display his wealth and power. Soon the decree came, a religious act, because the word *worship* is present 11 times in the story. King Nebuchadnezzar wanted his people to worship that image representative of himself.

In his desire to show the new idol off, the officials in the Babylonian family received an invitation to the dedication ceremony for which there was no RSVP. When the King sent an invitation, everyone was obligated to show up. Without the choice element, the word *invitation* should really be understood as *demand*.

This new rule that came out of the blue is revealed in Daniel 3:4-6 which says,

⁴Then a herald shouted out, "People of all races and nations and languages, listen to the king's command! ⁵When you hear the sound of the horn, flute, zither, lyre, harp, pipes, and other musical instruments, bow to the ground to worship King Nebuchadnezzar's gold statue. ⁶Anyone who refuses to obey will immediately be thrown into a blazing furnace." (NLT)

Three hundred thousand people were summoned by the King's orchestra. Although Daniel was not present due to other responsibilities, his three friends Shadrach, Meshach, and Abednego were on assignment at the ceremony. When the orchestra resumed, the three remained standing as the 300,000 other attendees lowered their heads to the ground.

The three Hebrews had a decision to make.

Would they defy and defile the Babylonian empire or would they maintain their allegiance to God?

Too often there are expectations of the world system clashing (such as the Babylonian empire at the time) with what we understand is our allegiance to God. When this happens we are stuck with a decision to make. It was an easy decision for the three Hebrews because they had made a decision of who they were and whose they were a long time before the moment they were asked to make this choice. They had been pledging their allegiance to God while in captivity a long time and they were not going to turn back now.

What doesn't make sense is the Chaldeans had no problem with the Hebrews' allegiance to God as long as they were benefiting from it. Think about how not long ago the same tattle tale Chaldean officials were the very same ones that Daniel and his friends had prayed for, and for whom Daniel intervened when the officials were about to lose their lives. I bet we can all relate to this. Think about how very little time it took for the Chaldean officials to transform themselves from beneficiaries to the very accusers of Shadrach, Meshach, and Abednego! (I have people like that in my story. I bet we all do.)

Many of us can relate to going along doing life the same way but the atmosphere or circumstances have shifted for no apparent reason, and we did not get the memo. Now what?

These officials shamelessly stood before the king and brought accusations against Shadrach, Meshach, and Abednego. They were accused of not respecting, nor paying regard, nor serving the King's gods. It was their refusal to worship the image that got them into trouble.

Daniel and his friends had previously been honored and promoted by the king; therefore, this king was put in a tough spot. The king gave the men a chance to compromise, but they refused. They knew compromising would go against everything they stood for. Shadrach, Meshach, and Abednego knew either their choice was to defy and defile the king, or Almighty God Himself. This choice is likely one we will visit sometime in our lives, maybe sooner rather than later.

These heroic men gave the king their answer in the most respectful manner possible. They told him they did not need to even consider the royal proposition. They had already made a decision in advance and there was no wavering. At this point is one of the most powerful declarations, most inspiring, and most motivational words ever known, and we have it recorded in Daniel 3:16-18:

¹⁶ Shadrach, Meshach, and Abednego replied, "O Nebuchadnezzar, we do not need to defend ourselves before you. ¹⁷ If we are thrown into the blazing furnace, the God whom we serve is able to save us. He will rescue us from your power, Your Majesty. ¹⁸ But even if he doesn't, we want to make it clear to you, Your Majesty, that we will never serve your gods or worship the gold statue you have set up." (NLT)

When they said, *but if not*, they were not questioning God's ability to deliver them. They were placing themselves in submission to God's will. They were saying it might not be the will of God to deliver them, but if not, it still made no difference. If it was not His will to deliver them, the Hebrews would accept that and glorify their God anyway.

In the *Exposition of Daniel*, Herbert C. Leupold writes, "The quiet, modest yet positive attitude of faith these three men display is one of noblest examples in the scriptures of being fully resigned to the will of God. These men ask for no miracle and they expect none. Theirs is the faith which says, "Though He slay me, yet will I trust Him..." (Job 13:15 KJV).

So often we want to make bargains with God. Do we not? There is no bargaining here. The men are not saying, "Lord if you do this, we'll do that." Rather, they are saying, "We're going to do this, and You do what You need to do."

These three guys raised the standard on taking a stand pretty high, did they not? They took a stand even though they knew it would land them in the fiery furnace. As Christians in today's culture, we may have to be prepared when we do stand, our faith may land us in the fiery furnace.

*****

What about the King's anger? He realized he was not going to control Shadrach, Meshach, and Abednego, or get what he wanted out of them. He was not going to be able to save face and keep the men alive, so he played his role up to his entire kingdom and decided to let them burn publically with a vengeance. It seems King Nebuchadnezzar was always running for election, constantly worried about his image. Why had he decided to turn the heat of the furnace up seven times hotter than usual? At this point, it had become personal. Still, the men did not fold under pressure and power.

It is terrible when people against us have the power and resources to decide our fate, and to determine the temperature in which we must face it. The strongest men in the king's army were summoned to bind the young men with ropes and cast them into the fire. They were bound in their clothes – coats, hats and other garments, which later becomes a glowing testimony to the deliverance of God.

The fiery furnace was so hot the only way the soldiers could get close enough to carry out their orders was to swing the three men toward the opening at the top of the furnace. Even then, the flames from the furnace fried the skin of the soldiers' bodies and they fell down dead after Shadrach, Meshach, and Abednego, bound hand and foot, plummeted into the blazing fire.

What would the king do now? Did somebody not follow his orders correctly? He positioned himself to check out personally what went wrong, which was when he identified the fourth man and said, "He is like the son of God."

No, he was not *like* the son of God. He *was* the Son of God.

Not *a* god, but *the* God.

*****

When the fourth man showed up in the flames, the event was what is known as Theophany, a visible manifestation of God, a clear manifestation of the Lord Jesus

Christ in the Old Testament. Amazingly, 580 years before the virgin birth, King Nebuchadnezzar saw the Lord Jesus Christ in the fiery furnace.

Notice God did not prevent the men from being thrown into the fire, but He showed up in there with them.

He's that God Whom can be with us when we are going *through* fire. He may not get us out of it but He will go through it with us.

Before we are threatened by fire, we have to determine in advance how we will respond under trial. The days of surface faith and cowardly Christianity are gone. We must realize being a Christian may soon cost more than many are willing to pay.

It's tempting to think we are far removed from the time when God's people would be thrown in a furnace, but a quick check in the headlines gives us the brutal truth every day. The world hates Christians, just as Jesus said. Yet, within opposition is an opportunity for the world to know God.

Shadrach, Meshach, and Abednego were able to testify before thousands of people because of their persecution. If you've asked Jesus to be your Savior, I pray your convictions are deeply held so you can display that kind of courage.

If further evidence is needed about the level of courage we need in today's culture, ask the people imprisoned for their faith. Ask those in leadership who take a stand for kingdom principles. Ask the politicians who refuse to turn heads.

Ready to recite the Overcomer's Creed?

> I will get through this because God is with me.
>
> My walk through fire may be painful,
>
> And it may be long,
>
> But with God's help I will overcome.
>
> In the meantime, I will be wise and hopeful because
>
> God will use IT for good.

THREE

Evil Intentions

Jealousy is often the root of an evil tapestry the enemy weaves to steal, kill and destroy.

— Dr. Lisa

Joseph's walk through fire, his *IT*, begins in a pit (Genesis 37), a dark pit so steep, so deep, that escape is impossible. We can imagine the rocks at the bottom and roots growing out of the side of this abandoned cistern. If we could peer over the pit to its bottom, we would see the 17-year-old boy. His hands are bound to his ankles, and he is lying on his side. His voice is hoarse from shouting and screaming but no one is listening. It is not that his brothers cannot hear him, but they choose not to do so.

Some two decades later Genesis 42:21 shows us they would confess "... We saw the anguish of his soul when he pleaded with us, and we would not hear..." (NKJV)

Who are these brothers?

They were the great grandsons of Abraham, the sons of Jacob. The ones for whom the 12 tribes were going to be named. In the book of Revelation, we are told that their names were engraved in the foundation of the gates of Jerusalem. So this is as close as the Bible gets to royalty. As author Max Lucado has said in his teaching series entitled, *You'll Get Through This*, "They were the Kennedy's of their day, yet a Bronze Aged dysfunctional family who could have their own TV reality show." They hated their brother so much that they threw him in a pit and then took off for lunch. While Joseph screamed for help, they nonchalantly had a meal together in oblivious hardhearted insensitivity.

Why?

Pure jealousy!

Their father Jacob pampered Joseph like a prize. Joseph was the son of Rachel, the wife he loved best. So, as Jacob's favorite son, Joseph got the best of everything from his father, which led to much brotherly hatred, emphasized several times throughout the story. His brothers could not speak peaceably about him. So finally, when they caught Joseph 60 miles away from their father's protection, they decided to put an end to him. They stripped his tunic and threw him in a pit. They were happy for the boy to die until they had an opportunity to profit from his life, and because their desire for money was just a little stronger than their desire for blood, they saw a chance to sell him into slavery.

Now Joseph did not see this assault coming, for he had not awakened that morning thinking, "I better put on my padded clothing because this is the day I get dumped in a pit!"

The attack caught him off guard, as did ours!

It always does, these attacks, these fires that seem to come out of nowhere.

Now Joseph's walk through fire began in the form of a cistern, and as it is for many of us, his story got worse before it got better. The abandonment led to enslavement, entrapment, and imprisonment. Joseph was sucker punched. He was mistreated time and time again. People broke their promises to him. They offered gifts to him, only to take them back. Yet Joseph never gave up. He *never* gave up.

Here was a guy who never got bitter lest his anger metastasize into hatred. He never let his heart get hard. There was something about his persona that enabled him not just to survive but also to thrive. In every stage of his life, Joseph was promoted to the top of the class. Yes, he was sold into slavery, but he was put in charge of Potiphar's household. Yes, he was incarcerated, but the next thing you know he was in charge of the prison. Yes, he was brought in front of Pharaoh, but Pharaoh appointed him the prime minister. By the end of his life, this boy in the pit was the prince in the palace and responsible for distributing food at one of the most difficult times in human history. It is hardly exaggeration to say that Joseph saved an entire generation from starvation. Joseph saved the world. That's pretty impressive for a kid whose story begins in the depths of a pit. How did he do it?

We do not have to speculate. He gave us the answer. Many years later, when the roles were reversed and the brothers were the ones in trouble, Joseph was the one in charge. His brothers came to him pleading for mercy because they were afraid they were going to end up in a pit of Joseph's making. Still, Genesis 50:20 illustrates Joseph telling them, "²⁰ As for you, you meant evil against me, but God meant it for good, to bring it about that many people[a] should be kept alive, as they are today." (ESV)

You meant evil against me but God meant it for good. Now that word *meant* comes out of the Hebrew language. It means to weave. Weave *something*. If we were to weave a tapestry, we might use this word. In essence, Joseph told them that they came weaving evil – taking the threads of evil and weaving them together. But God took their same threads and re-wove them into a *good* tapestry. Evil had been brought into his life but God re-wove it into something good.

*****

I have extensive experience with someone weaving a tapestry of evil and using it for destruction. As you remember in my series of *ITs,* I shared the legal battles I had with the school that I started and the criminal accusations the State of Ohio auditor's office made against the board and the staff of the school where I was the Chief Executive Officer. As it was with Joseph, the root of evil against us started with jealousy.

Back in 2006, there was a lady (for these purposes we will call Jean) the treasurer hired to help in the accounting department at the school. Jean had been through difficult times and had just lost a big executive job and needed employment. Jean attended church with the school treasurer and was a "so called" friend of hers, but over time her level of appreciation of the job dissipated and she became jealous of the treasurer. Jean began misplacing her personal pain and hurting others by telling vicious rumors about employees. She resented the staff incentives some received such as paid continued education and planted seeds of dissension. Jean eventually had another job opportunity and moved out of state, but when that job did not work out for her, she attempted to return six months later and expected her old accounting job to still be available. When it was not, Jean retaliated and made a false fraud claim by contacting the state auditors department as a whistleblower. There were no whistles to be blown, but the false claims launched an enormous investigation. This was easy to do given the already hostile climate education reform (charter schools) created in the state of Ohio, which caused an enormity of destruction in the perfect storm.

Jealousy is often the root of an evil tapestry the enemy weaves to steal, kill, and destroy. Jealousy was in fact the root of this evil tapestry woven against me just as it was with Joseph's brothers. The jealousy among Joseph's brothers likely started with one brother in particular who influenced the other brothers.

Satan knows the weakest link, and if there is not a particular weak link, he can wear people down over time until they become weak enough to use for his purposes to steal, kill, and destroy. Jean was the vessel the enemy started with to weave an evil tapestry of destruction, but it did not end with her.

Over time, one part of the evil web was the creation of very extensive false narratives, enough ammunition to get a prosecutor to bring criminal charges against the leadership of the school. Eventually, they whittled the targets down to be just me the CEO by intimidating and manipulating others to take some type of deal. In the legal world, a common phrase is that a ham sandwich can be prosecuted, no pun intended, meaning that anybody can be charged with anything anywhere.

All the prosecutor has to do is hold a grand jury hearing and tell volunteer jurors his side of the evidence. There is no one representing the defendant. Even if the prosecutor presents erroneous information, the grand jury agrees to prosecute most of the time. It is a rare occasion that they do not. For those people without resources to defend themselves, things are much bleaker.

*****

We are finding now that at least 50% of people in our country will need legal help this year alone and the amount is rising. Therefore, I'll share a little more detail about the conundrum the entire legal process ended up being by giving you one example of the lack of common sense and the depth of the deceit that occurred. You never know, it may help prepare you in some way for some legal matter brought against you or someone within your circle of influence one day. And before thinking about legal action against the people that carried out this wrong doing, (governmental agencies, prosecutor's office working with governmental agencies,) forget about it because they have what is called "sovereign immunity." This means they can do whatever they want to whomever they want and you can do nothing about it. You can try but the chances of finding an attorney to take this on and having the resources to do so are slim to none.

There were so many different accusations over many years, and we were successful in disproving them, but eventually the auditors made something stick. They ended up accusing us of misspending public funds. It was as if they had never seen anyone add value, show appreciation, or to develop staff members and enrich students culturally. These people come from a mentality where generosity and appreciation is shown only when people have worked 30 years to retirement before they receive a watch.

Auditors reported that the team building and the student and staff incentives the school was giving was not a proper public purpose, which they deemed as a type of theft. For example, the board approved an administrative team of women to attend "A Graduate Course in Living Your Best Life," sponsored by *O* magazine, a personal development conference in Boston, Massachusetts in 2006. Because the conference was approved by the board and clearly on the books, how could that be theft, we might ask? The auditors were claiming the board was misled about the intent of the conference because they were told it was a graduate course as was clearly written in the board minutes. I wondered myself why that would have been stated, so I began to investigate. It was difficult because the event took place in October of 2006 and I was reviewing this claim in 2012, six years after the fact. When I contacted *O* magazine, the entire marketing department in New York City looked into the old archives, until finally they located the documentation. We discovered that the title of the conference was advertised as "a graduate course in living your best life."

We're offering a graduate course in living your best life.

Meet a few of our professors.

In Boston on October 7 we're bringing O, The Oprah Magazine to life. Martha Beck, Suze Orman and Dr. Robin Smith are just three of the many contributors who will be gathered under one roof for a day of workshops and more. If you're ready for your best life to come to life, you won't want to miss out.

Registration begins August 21. Log on to Omagazine.info for more details.

What I had actually done was to get approval for the conference by using its exact title. The auditors used the facts to weave a web to misrepresent my intent. I had not misled anyone to get them to approve the expenses for the conference, but I was going to have to prove it. The auditors had woven a tapestry of false accusations like people would not believe unless they had been through it themselves.

Are our heads hurting yet? The prosecutor brought two charges against me for this conference. There were at least 12 other items like the aforementioned ones that led to 26 different charges designed to overwhelm the defense, so we would give up. Ridiculous. The length of time in dealing with them was worse. The conference was in October of 2006, and the charges were brought against me in February of 2013.

It took the auditors all of these years to weave this tapestry of evil, but they were okay with the time because the entire period they were collecting a paycheck from the government that eventually ended up on the school tab. The auditors collected well over $500K in fees from the school, which created great financial distress along with the legal fees. While I was serving as Superintendent of an inner city school, trying to minister to people, address the problems of society, raise student achievement, problem solve financial issues they had created, and attempt to maintain excellence in the three organizations I developed and built up to a success, they were weaving this evil tapestry. They were finding a way to justify their own wrongdoing and how many resources they were wasting. Most successful organizations deem team building and incentives as necessary, especially in high challenge work places. However, the opinions of the auditors allowed their investigative offices to deem these actions as criminal.

Over time, one part of the evil web was to take five years of audits of the school and add all of the team building and incentive fund allocations together, which largely inflated the amount of money spent on them. And then they started selling it to the public across the airwaves. The school had a 7 million dollar budget each year and at most there were $50,000 spent in these areas annually (most of it having been raised from outside revenue). These expenses did not benefit me personally but those at the school. Yet, within the evil tapestry, a complete fabrication of the truth was woven.

Why did the auditors not tell the truth on this about the fact that most of the funds were not public monies? Because they discovered this fact while preparing for trial, and they did not want to acknowledge the oversight. At this point, the issue had become personal for them. They had invested so much and had sown so many evil threads in the tapestry. They were exhilarated with all of this, and they were going to really show their value to the public. Sadly, bureaucrats like this believe they are doing a good thing. Some receive promotions and financial increases.

Probably the most heart wrenching phenomenon was that over time one part of the evil web was to divide the very close-knit, family oriented people of God at the school, so that I, the CEO, could be an easy target for attack and destruction. Over time, each individual involved in the school, whether it be a staff member or board member was questioned, interrogated, hounded, and manipulated until they no longer supported me. Those who remained supportive had their positions terminated and were threatened with criminal charges. A pastor that served as a board member was questioned and when he told the truth and told investigators in the auditor's office that board members always approved and participated in the items that were in question, and provided a statement to the effect, and showed board minutes proving it, he was harassed by investigators in the auditor's office at home and work and was called before the grand jury. He nearly lost his second job he was working at and it severed our relationship. All parties who revoked their support from me were given some type of deal to cooperate with the auditors. They were made to go against me out of fear, and I guess self preservation. This tapestry of evil broke the cords of unity among the staff in service to God and destroyed lifelong relationships.

*****

The evil tapestry woven seemed iron clad and played out well against me. Along the way, I was educated about the depth of the scheme and the dangerous political chess game into which I was thrown.

It was like a dance of the lemons with the attorney's themselves throughout the life of the case, beginning with the school attorney. I worked closely with the school attorney since the school opened in 1999. Not only did this attorney supply the school policies and advise me over a decade on all of these matters which ended up being related to the case, she participated in the activities at least annually over a decade. Once the charges were filed against us, she conveniently began representing the immunized board members because it was more lucrative for her and a better career opportunity. Even though it was clearly a conflict of interest that she was represent immunized board members who approved school policies she designed, which were part of my defense, she did it anyway and got away with it.

This attorney advised we get additional legal counsel support so we did and sent someone from a downtown firm the school was working with for real estate issues. This particular attorney, early on in the defense, told me that he and the school attorney agreed the issue was political and that I needed to approach the resolution a different way. He said that I should contribute funds to a particular candidate running for state auditor in the election. He said if I gave a certain dollar amount to this campaign that I would have the ability to discuss the issue with this candidate when elected and it would be resolved. I did contribute to the campaign but this person was not elected. He was however elected to another high office. Realize the disappointment I felt when I discovered this attorney, acting as if he was helping me, was the campaign manager for the person running for state auditor. He was using this legal situation to benefit the campaign instead of really helping. Needless to say, we soon realized this was the wrong attorney and began trying to find the right one.

We had a visit at the school by a former city councilman that had been a supporter of school reform who was also a lawyer. When I shared what we were facing he set up a meeting with me, the school treasurer, and the board chair and a different downtown law firm. After the consultation, this attorney and the firm itself began representing the school, the treasurer and me, the superintendent in what was now deemed a criminal defense. Later after these attorneys dragged the case on for two years, we discovered it was a conflict of interest to have them represent all parties. From this point they began representing me and the treasurer, staff members, and board members each obtained other different legal counsel even though the entire time we worked on the defense and share all documentation preparing for the defense that I personally put together. After the entire defense was prepared by me and after I prepared a huge document for cross examination of every party related to every charge against us (me and the treasurer at this point), these attorneys withdrew the case on the day set for trial. They had already collected all of the legal fees and I had no more financial resources, while being threatened with losing my entire retirement pension. These attorneys ended up withdrawing from the case without ever doing anything after having collected at least $145,000 from all of us together. When they withdrew, I had no money for another attorney. At this point, I was manipulated into a plea deal that ended up being a lie. (More on this later.)

Bottom line, when people tell you to do whatever your attorney says, make sure you seek other wise counsel or you will be disappointed later.

Part of the education I received may shock most of us naïve to the legal system. First in dealing with the legal system realize everything is a game or performance. The players within the system approach it like a game of pickup basketball and "win some you lose some" attitudes are prevalent. There is very little concern to what will happen with the lives of those who are vulnerable to the actions of the system. The truth does not matter. Only perceptions and narratives created based on those perceptions matter.

Nearly everything that is decided in the court room goes on behind the scenes.

All players go into the judge's chambers and then when in the court room they simply perform. At times opposing sides even help one another with presentations but when in public they act as if they are in opposition, but it is really an act.

You see, the attorneys on both sides are all friends and colleagues and most often times the actions they take and deals they make do not have to do with the clients they represent. It has to do with what the best opportunity is for them at the time. And if they can cause a case to drag on in order to gain more financially, that is what they do regardless of what happens to lives of those who will be affected. It is scary! The only person surprised about what happens in the court room is the client.

*****

God did give me aid along the way. I was supported by one particularly astute young man named Aaron who stood in to speak for me and attempted to inform people of the truth behind the matters and common errors made by government. It was like God sent me an angel. If he had not gone into military service right thereafter, I would have believed he was an angel. Even some politicians began to investigate on my behalf only to find that the heat was soon turned on them. Aaron even approached the governor's office at the time only to find he would not get involved. The governor was under fire with the auditor's office at the time for a job's bill. Later I found out this governor was not going to do anything to help. (Interestingly enough, he is currently running for president.)

Clearly, the force behind this evil tapestry had power and position not just to cause harm to me, but to many others, so people over time just began to turn their heads.

How could any person, or group of people, devise such a scheme and take so much time and effort to carry it out?

Joseph's brothers certainly did this, and so I imagine Joseph had the same questions. Someone wanted me completely out of the way. The brothers wanted Joseph out of the way and we can see how evil their hearts had become by the way they did it. They allowed Joseph to be taken captive as a slave because they knew they were benefiting from it. They got money from the sale, and they no longer were going to have to compete for their father's attention. Their brother's loss was their gain. Everything would now belong to them. Joseph was out of the way for good.

*****

Satan is the source of this evil, and his logic is simple as it related to Joseph. If he can destroy the family of Abraham, well, he can destroy the lineage of Jesus Christ, and so he came in weaving evil. He wanted to destroy the family of Abraham, the sons of Jacob, but God took the very actions of evil and re-wove them in such a fashion that He promoted one of the sons of Jacob to be Prime Minister so that the family was not destroyed. It was just the opposite. The descendants of Abraham ended up in a protective place in Egypt with Joseph on the throne. Who would have thought? What was intended as evil God used for good to protect all of these people.

Do you know the reason I think that Joseph's story is in the Bible? I believe it is there to teach us that God can TRUMP any evil in the world. No pun intended. (If you are reading this book and are not from America you may not understand the joke, so I will explain. It is election season 2016 and one of the candidates running for the presidential election is Donald Trump.)

*****

There is nothing in the story of Joseph that would say there is no evil in the world.

Evil is on every page. There is evil on every corner of the world today.

But every page, even every paragraph, every sentence in the story of Joseph tells us that God can take this evil that has come into our world and use it.

He can reroute *IT*.

He can re-weave *IT*.

He can re-purpose *IT*.

He can recycle IT.

He can redeem *IT* into something good.

To borrow the phrases from Max Lucado's *You'll Get Through This* teaching series, We are going to get through this. We are. We are going to get through this. Yet we fear we won't.

That's one of the challenges of tough times. We fear the depression will never lift. We fear the screaming will never stop. We fear we will never understand the pain. We fear we will not get through it. We need to know that *through* is one of God's favorite words.

He gets us *through* the Red Sea.

He gets us *through* the storm.

He gets us *through* the fiery furnace.

We are in a hurry and often late. But God is always on time. So if God is taking His time that's okay.

God will use this fire, this trial, tribulation, obstacle or this perfect mess. We look at Joseph in the pit and we say, "What a mess!" But God looks at it and says, "What a perfect opportunity. This is a perfect chance to train and develop the future Prime Minister of Egypt!"

I do not know everything Joseph needed to learn. But God knew exactly what Joseph needed to learn, and part of that training came in the pit, part of it came in the house of Potiphar, and part of that training came in the prison.

All those travails were working together to create the kind of person whom God was going to use to accomplish His will.

God is working right now in this mess, this fire.

He is working right now in the chaos and confusion.

He is teaching us something He wants us to know.

He is training us. For what I cannot say, God can. He has us enrolled right now in a course for which perhaps we did not volunteer. Still, it is an assigned curriculum from the Creator of the Universe. He has assigned us this curriculum because He wants us to develop a characteristic or two that He can then use to further His Kingdom.

Again, the story of Joseph is in the Bible to teach us that God trumps evil, even the worst kind of evil.

Let's do it.

I will get through this because God is with me.

My walk through fire may be painful,

And it may be long,

But with God's help I will overcome.

In the meantime, I will be wise and hopeful because

God will use IT for good.

*For more study on the trust, discernment, betrayal and leadership, and spiritual covering see the *Walking Through Fire* Bible Study Series.

FOUR

Destiny Deferred

Nobody can take our destiny, and part of reaching our destiny is understanding the detours. Attacks do not kill dreams. They deter them. Only a lack of continual pursuit can kill our dreams!

-Dr. Lisa

Eighteen-year-old Cory Weissman was a star basketball player on his way to the top. He scored 1000 points in his high school career, earning a seat on the Gettysburg College basketball team. He kept his body in tip top shape and worked vigorously towards achieving his goals until the day that everything came crashing down. He suffered a significant AVM stroke and doctors were not sure he was going to make it through the night. Cory survived but was paralyzed on his left side. He questioned why such a terrible thing happened and felt he did not deserve it.

Still, he was determined to get his dream back. He began the long grueling process of physical therapy with the expectation of a full recovery so that he could once again play basketball. He made great progress, but the brain damage caused ongoing seizures that made his dream unreachable. His dream of playing college basketball was gone, and now his life would never be the same. Cory's dream was deferred.

What happens to a dream deferred?

Does it dry up like a raisin in the sun,

Or fester like a sore –

and then run?

Does it stink like rotten meat – or crust in sugar over like a syrupy sweet,

Maybe it just sags like a heavy load-

or does it explode?

This poem by Langston Hughes best expresses the sentiment Solomon had in Proverbs 13:12: "Hope deferred makes the heart sick, but a longing fulfilled is the tree of life" (NIV).

After nearly one year of raising three children as my own, whom I was soon expecting to adopt, in one afternoon, they were abruptly taken back to their biological father. Although I was happy to know the children's biological father was ready to get his life together again, the loss of the children was a big hit. I had been given false hope and my dreams for motherhood were gone. After three years of fighting cancer with my father, only to have the battle end in death, was a big hit. My dream for his health and life being restored was gone. After 15 years of building successful schools in the inner city, seeing my students thrive, seeing my staff members grow into amazing educators, and seeing a neighborhood transformed from a place of doom to a place of vibrancy, only to have it all stolen from me was a big hit. My dream for doing even greater things as an educator for this community was destroyed.

This is certainly a dream deferred for my life, but because I experienced so much loss and change in such a short time, it has felt like more than just a dream deferred. It has felt like my entire destiny had been deferred. I was no longer a mother, no longer someone's daughter, and no longer a superintendent or educator. I was left without a sense of destiny, a sense of knowing the purpose of my life, I have questioned how I would survive. I have wondered if I would even enjoy my life again. A counselor I was seeing told me I was experiencing the same thing soldiers of war face when they come home from military service and try to assimilate in society but cannot. They, like me, have very specialized training and when they cannot use it, they are lost. Their sense of destiny is lost.

I imagine Joseph felt that too. He certainly did not deserve what happened to him. He was abandoned by his brothers, sold as a slave, and put in prison. Yet he survived.

Not only did he survive but he thrived.

One of the best questions we can ask is this: How do we explain Joseph's survival? How do we explain his success? Do we notice the Bible never says anything about his education or his training? It never says anything about Joseph's skills or talents. All the Bible gives us when it comes to Joseph going into Egypt are those mysterious dreams, the dreams. You see, those dreams were more to Joseph then mere images in the night. Something about these dreams convinced Joseph that God had a plan.

All Joseph had when he arrived in Egypt was a sense of God's hand upon him. Joseph knew that God had a special place for him, a special use for him. That is all Joseph had and in the end that is all Joseph needed.

The word we use to describe a gift like this is destiny.

Destiny.

Regardless of what circumstances he was going through, Joseph maintained a sense of destiny for his life.

I can just picture him being led across the desert thinking, *Okay there's more to my life than this.* God, what about the dream you showed me? How is my life going to work out into me becoming a leader when I'm being sold into slavery?

I'd like to talk about destiny.

Do we have a sense of destiny in our lives?

I have heard many anecdotes of how people have been taken down the road to Egypt (gone into the fire) with their own challenges and calamities, and I have learned a good question to ask individuals passing through a time like this, a *walk through fire*. I would ask this: What is the one thing we still have that no one can take?

No one diminishes the fact, my friend, that life takes much from us.

Life takes opportunities. Life takes our health. Life takes our loved ones and our friends, but the aforementioned question is a good one. What is the one gift, the one element of our lives that no one can touch? The answer to that question is God's destiny. No one can touch it.

People can take a lot of things from us, and life does take a lot of things, but no one can take our destinies.

I heard it said best from a message by Jentzen Franklin, Senior Pastor of Free Chapel in Gainesville, Georgia called "The God of What's Left." Franklin argued, "We know He is the God of our blessings and that all good things come from Him. But I want you to understand He is also God of what is lost, and that's not all. When life, sickness, or death takes from you and your family, His purpose for you is not over … He's *The God of What's Left!*"

*****

In many ways, Tommy Dorsey's story is that of a modern day Joseph. Dorsey was born in 1899, the son of a Baptist pastor and a pianist. He became quite a talented musician and became known in jazz circles as "Georgia Tom," but when he gave his life to Christ at age 22, he began writing hymns and leading worship. But then one evening the fire came. When he was in St. Louis, he was just about to step up and lead worship in a congregation when somebody stepped onto the platform and handed Dorsey a telegram about the sudden death of his wife. While giving birth to their newborn son, his wife Nettie had died. Tommy rushed to the hospital in a panic and held back the grief of her death so that he could tend to the needs of his newborn baby, but his baby ended up dying within the next 24 hours.

As often is the case, the crisis led to a crisis of faith.

Dorsey began to struggle. How could God let this happen after all he had given up, and all the good decisions he had made, and all the things he had done? How could God let this happen? Dorsey went into a crevice of discouragement and depression, and he vowed that he would never write another hymn. It was hard. It was so hard.

A friend of his at a music school with a small campus invited Dorsey to come and spend a few days on the campus. There, he could surround himself with music away from his responsibilities. Dorsey took his friend up on the offer. One evening as Dorsey was walking through one of the buildings, he saw a room that had a piano in it, so he walked in. There was the piano with nobody in the room. The sun was setting, and there was something about that moment that led him to play and to pray for the first time in a long time. He began to pour his heart out to God. He began to ask God for help and for strength. He wrote a song that night: "Precious Lord, take my hand, lead me on, let me stand, I am tired, I am weak, I am worn. Through the storm, through the night, lead me on to the light, take my hand precious Lord, lead me home."

For the rest of his life, Dorsey testified that the Lord healed him that night as he sat at the piano. Here he was as a young man, and later in life he would write more than 3000 songs and become one of the most influential songwriters in all of history. He is now known as the "Father of Gospel Music."

He could have made another choice, could he not? He could have walked away, but he made a difference because he made a decision to come back to God. We are all going to pass through tough times. My prayer is that during our tough times we will do what Joseph did, what Thomas A. Dorsey did. We will do what God wants us to do. We will not be foolish. We will not be naïve, but we will reach out and take God's hand. We will trust that the One who was let us go so far, will be the One to lead us home.

Now destiny has come to us in a variety of ways. It differs depending on our skills, our talents, and our history, but there are a couple of common denominators in all of our destinies. Number one, we are God's children. Before we are anything, we are God's children. Before we are male or female, Asian or Hispanic, we are God's children. This means He chose us. He purchased us. He laid claim to us when he said, "I want you to be a part of my eternal kingdom." Nobody can take that from us. They can take just about anything from us but nobody can take away this simple truth. We have got to hang onto it like the safety net that it is. Nobody can take our destiny, and part of reaching our destiny is understanding the detours. Attacks do not kill dreams. They deter them. Only a lack of continual pursuit can kill our dreams!

We are His children for all eternity even unto death. We must not believe the tombstone that starts with a date, has a dash in between, and then ends in a date.

*****

I shared my series of *IT*s in chapter one. The loss of my close childhood friend Rita's life was one of those *IT*s. Rita was diagnosed with a debilitating form of cancer in her mid-forties. When this happened, almost daily we walked the track and neighborhood of the small town of Ludlow, Kentucky we grew up in to keep our bodies strong and to support each other by sharing the struggles we were facing in life. Rita was married and a mother of two teenage children. She was fighting for her life, not solely for her own well being but for the well being of her family. We find that people who are dying tend not to fear death but are more concerned for the well being of those they leave behind. I did not want to believe that Rita was dying, but over time the evidence grew that her body could no longer function properly and rapid changes began taking place. As a person of faith, even though Rita knew she was going to soon leave this world, she somehow maintained a sense of comfort in that she still had a destiny. A destiny set for her that was much better than what this world could offer and a destiny that no sickness could ever take again.

As a follower of Jesus Christ, Rita knew two things for certain. One was that if she died,

God would watch over her family. And secondly, was that if she died and she closed her eyes in this world, she would open her eyes in the presence of God Himself.

One day we all will sooner or later come to a day that will end in tragedy. Many people fear this so much, that people cannot even face the thought of it. They are afraid of the pain, the unknown, and being separated from loved ones. They cannot fathom the thought of death.

If there is any time we need hope it is when we face death. More and more people in our culture are asking the same question that Job asked so long ago in Job 14:14, "If someone dies, will they live again?... (NIV)"

Is that not the most important question of all?

I love what Jesus said to Martha after the death of Lazarus, her brother and Jesus' friend. Jesus said, "I am the resurrection and the life. The one who lives in me will live, even though they die." (John 11:25 NIV)

In other words Jesus said, there is life after death. My followers can be confident that they will conquer the grave. The tombstone says we started at this date and ended at another date and in between we are just a tiny dash, yet according to God, we are His children forever.

I love this verse from the apostle Paul in 2 Corinthians 5:1 which says, "For we know that if the earthly tent [our physical body] which is our house is torn down [through death], we have a building from God, a house not made with hands, eternal in the heavens." (AMP)

So we must not get sucked into this short-term thinking. God has a great plan for us. This destiny means that God's greatest plan lies ahead for us. God's greatest plans for us are literally out of this world. They are out of this life, they are in the next life and everything in this life is working together to prepare us for what lies ahead. This is God's destiny that nobody can take from us.

I really think Joseph must have known this because when he arrived in Egypt, he did not have anything else. He did not have money, clothing, friends, or clout, but it was just a matter of time before God took all that was intended for evil and turned it in something good. He could do this in Joseph's life because Joseph trusted the destiny that God had for him.

*****

How can we follow in the example of Joseph and maintain a sense of destiny when we have incurred such loss?

Because we believe the promises of God and God promises to give us abundant life.

Abundant life is a fun life. It is a play-filled life. How can we walk in such a life as this after we have gone through the fire? How can we depend on this when we are still in the fire?

We can because it is a promise of God, but as Dr. Mark Chironna has said, "You can't step out on a promise and walk into a future by gravitating back to an old normal that you used to walk in before you went through your valley of shadows. What you were doing before you went through that valley was your old normal, you can't go back there. It doesn't exist anymore. God is cutting you off from that in this season. Your new normal doesn't represent or resemble your old normal in any way shape or form, and it is not supposed to, because you have changed at a very profound level. You are not the same person you were before you went through that valley. You are deeply shifting in terms of who you are, where you have been, and where you are going."

Joseph was never going to go back to being the little brother favored by his father. If he knew what God had in store for him in his role as Prime Minister of Egypt, he would not have wanted to anyway. He was not the same person. His fire experience melted him down so much that he was made into some new thing.

After the fire experience, we have changed. We are not the same people! We have been melted down under extreme temperatures to some new thing that we do not yet recognize.

Now we are asked to trust again at a whole new level. We are being asked to believe a promise of a future destiny, yet in order to walk in it; we cannot rely on the way we have been used to walking before. We feel like our steps are uncertain and we feel vulnerable and uncertain in faith.

The life of Joseph shows us we are in great company but we also must remember his great grandfather Abraham. God says to Abraham, "...Leave your country, leave your relatives, and leave your father's house. Go to the land I will show you" (Genesis 12:1 NLT).

Abraham went out not knowing where he was going; however, he knew what he was looking for. He knew he was looking for a city. He knew he was looking for a seed. He knew he was looking for multiplication. He knew he was looking for the dominion mandate to be renewed in his children and his children's children.

We are walking out, walking on, walking beyond in vulnerable faith, uncertain of where we are going. We have to step out on a promise of God to walk into a future destiny and we must refuse to look in the rear view mirror.

When we start stepping out into this future destiny for the first time in our lives, we are going to come to the realization that the journey of faith is never ending. As people of faith, we must be comfortable with walking in uncertainty, because uncertainty is the atmosphere in which the promise will manifest. In our lives there are generations of possibility, promise, and glory that will be released.

This season God is healing us of our disappointments and renewing us by the spirit in His promises (2 Peter 1: 4) to make us partakers of the divine nature of Jesus, because it is time for us to possess our possessions. Resurrection life flows through the depths of our beings (Romans 8:11). The same spirit that raised Jesus from the dead dwells in us, and He is going to quicken us! We must step out on His promises. We must walk in to our future destinies!

Let say our Overcomer's Creed:

> I will get through this because God is with me.
>
> My walk through fire may be painful,
>
> And it may be long,
>
> But with God's help I will overcome.
>
> In the meantime, I will be wise and hopeful because
>
> God will use *IT* for good.

*For more study on dreams and destiny see the *Walking Through Fire* Bible Study Series.

FIVE

A Hint from Heaven

Until God provides direction, I look for a hint from heaven in the most trying times.

— Dr. Lisa

In *Man's Search for Meaning,* Holocaust survivor and renowned psychologist Victor Frankl's written account is less about his travails, what he suffered and lost, than it is about the source of his strength to survive. While Frankl was held captive in the death camps and stripped of everything he loved, including his family, he decided to use the experience as a laboratory. He talks about prisoners who gave up on life, who lost all hope for the future, and who were inevitably the first to die. They died less from lack of food or medicine than from lack of hope, lack of something to live for.

Frankl kept his hope alive by summoning up thoughts of love and purpose. He thought of the love of his wife and the prospect of seeing her again, and dreamed at one point of lecturing after the war about the psychological lessons to be learned from the Auschwitz experience. Clearly, many prisoners who desperately wanted to live did die, some from disease, some in the crematoria. But Frankl's concern is less with the question of why most died than it is with the question of why anyone survived at all.

Horrific as it was, Frankl's experience in Auschwitz reinforced what was already a key idea: life is not primarily a quest for pleasure or for power, as many scholars have believed, but a quest for meaning. The greatest task for anyone is to find meaning in his or her life. Frankl saw three possible sources for meaning: working to do something significant, love and caring for another person, and giving encouragement during difficult times.

Frankl explains that suffering in and of itself is meaningless; we give our suffering meaning by the way we respond to it. At one point, Frankl writes that while a person may remain brave, dignified, and unselfish, or in the bitter fight for self-preservation, he may forget his human dignity and become no more than an animal. He concedes that only a few prisoners of the Nazis were able to remain brave, dignified, and unselfish, but even one such example is sufficient proof that man's inner strength may raise him above his outer fate.

Finally, Frankl's most enduring insight is forces beyond our control can take away everything we possess except for one thing, our freedom to choose how to respond to the situation. We cannot control what happens to us in our life, yet we can always control what we will feel and do about what happens to us. Frankl would believe that we are never left with nothing as long as we retain the freedom to choose how we will respond.

Frankl insists that life is meaningful and that we must learn to see such meaningfulness despite our circumstances. He emphasizes that there is an ultimate purpose to life. The original version of *Man's Search for Meaning*, before a postscript was added to his book, concluded with one of the most profoundly written sentences written in the 20th century: "We have come to know man as he really is. After all, man is that being who invented the gas chambers of Auschwitz; however, he is also that being who entered those gas chambers upright, with the Lord's Prayer or the Schema Yisrael on his lips."

*****

I have been asked why I was not able to prevent things from happening in my walk through fire. Why did not I get issues resolved before they snowballed out of control? How did I not know that the auditors had a secret criminal investigation going on behind my back the entire time they were at the school six months or more? Why had I kept the chief finance officer in place if duties were not being completed to the satisfaction of the auditors?

To answer all of these questions: *I do not know*. I did the best I could with what I knew at the time. Decision-making in life is so important, and in many respects, throughout the time that I ran the school, and throughout other times in my life, I made the wrong decisions. But one thing is for sure – I have always done my best. I never had an intention to do wrong in my adult life and certainly not in my leadership role. Every decision that I made was for the benefit of my students, the families of my students, the community, the teachers, and the administrators and staff at the school.

People mean well by asking these questions, but they fail to recognize we have already asked ourselves the same questions repeatedly, so we do not need help in beating ourselves up. Really what they are saying when they ask such questions is how could I have made so many stupid mistakes, or how could I have been so powerless under the circumstances? The good thing about this crisis is that I learned more during this time than in any other time of my life. I learned more than I did in all my formal education through my bachelor's, my master's, and my PhD degrees. I learned more than I did in starting my grassroots businesses, two schools, a preschool, and a professional development company. Rather than focus on things that I cannot change, I would rather focus on what I've learned and how I can help others in their lives from the lessons I have learned, the trauma I have experienced, and in what I believe is in our future based on what has happened in my past. What helped me resolve these issues was to think about people who had circumstances much worse than one could imagine, such as Victor Frankl.

In the middle of all the trauma, I read the *Man's Search for Meaning* again and I noticed that Frankl was faced with questions about why he did not try to escape what was in store for him after Hitler had occupied Austria.

Before the United States entered World War II, Victor Frankl received an invitation to come to the American consulate in Vienna to pick up his immigration visa. His parents were overjoyed because they expected that they would soon be allowed to leave Austria. Frankl, however, did not really feel he could afford to leave his parents alone to face their fate, to be sent, sooner or later, to a concentration camp. He thought about where his responsibility lay. He thought perhaps he should focus on his psychology work on logotherapy and write his books. He thought he could concentrate on his duties to protect his parents. Frankl's dilemma was one in which he should have wished for "a hint from heaven." It was just then that he noticed a piece of marble lying on a table at his home. He asked his father about it, and his father explained that he found it on the site where the national Socialists had burned down the largest PNE synagogue. His father had taken the piece with him because it was a part of the tablets on which the 10 Commandments were inscribed. One gilded Hebrew letter was engraved on the piece; his father explained that the letter stood for one of the commandments. When Victor Frankl asked which commandment it was, his father answered, "Honor thy father and thy mother that thy days may be long upon the land." At that moment, Frankl decided to stay with his father and mother upon the land, and to let the American visa lapse. That decision to stay with his parents is the one that caused him to suffer three grueling years of inhumane treatment. It was beyond what any of us could comprehend. He was sent to a concentration camp for Jewish prisoners under conditions that we have now named the Holocaust.

I relate to this story because the most extreme example of human cruelty did not stop people from asking prisoners like Victor Frankl stupid questions. How could I expect that people would not ask me these questions as well?

The point is, evil is evil and it does not care who it touches or how it gets to us. The source of evil in this world is Satan himself, and he will do what he can and use whomever he can to accomplish his mission: to steal, to kill, and to destroy. Not only has he attempted to do this by putting my light out and thwarting the purpose of God in my life as an educator in the inner-city, but with the exception of writing this book I have been very unproductive for the Kingdom of God because of what the enemy has been able to do. I have been looking for direction from God on where I should go and what I should do that He may be glorified most from my challenging circumstances. Until God provides direction, I look for a hint from heaven in the most trying times. The Bible says God is always speaking, so that must mean at times we just do not hear Him, or we think we hear Him but we are not certain of what it is we do hear.

*****

Priscilla Shirer highlighted the various methods God has used to speak to his people in *Discerning the Voice of God*. In this book, Shirer demonstrates that God's methods of speaking have changed throughout centuries but his goal of wanting His children to hear, recognize, and obey His voice have remained the same. Reflecting back on the examples in Bible, God has spoken to His people in many incredible ways:

- A burning bush (Exodus 3:4) and burning hearts (Luke 24:32)
- His glory (Numbers 14:22) and His humiliation (Philippians 2:8)
- A fire (Deuteronomy 5:24) and a cloud (Matthew 17:5)
- His name (Joshua 9:9) and His creation (Romans 1:20)
- Visible signs (Judges 6:40) and an invisible spirit (Matthew 10:20)
- Visions (Psalms 89:19) and dreams (Matthew 2:12)
- Teachers (Ecclesiastes 1:1) and evangelists (Acts 8:35)
- Angels (Daniel 8:15) and apostles (2Peter 3:2)

How do we know that what we are sensing within is actually the voice of God because our souls (mind, will, and emotions) and our spirits are slowly changing? We have influences all around us from a worldly culture, and we still carry baggage from sin, or just the damage life brings. How can we retain the confidence in our abilities to hear God?

God put a salvation plan in place to give us life in the spirit when we ask Jesus to be our Lord and Savior. He put a sanctification plan in place that awakens our conscience to walk out our lives. He knows we are not good listeners and that there are many distractions, so when God speaks individually to us, He repeats it more than once in different ways so we know it is He who is speaking.

God does not want us to miss Him. If we need more certainty we need just ask, "God I'm not sure what you are saying to me right now, but could you speak to me and give me clear direction on this matter?" This idea applies not only to the major decisions we need to make, but also to the smaller details of life.

Our lives are always a work in progress, but our experiences of correctly hearing God can lead us to be more certain that we are discerning correctly.

If not certain, I keep seeking. As we walk through our lives, regardless of the season, we should take note of the six "C's" that I believe will help us accurately discern God's voice that have been adapted from a list created by Priscilla Shirer:

Conviction of conscience. There is a knowing in our innermost spirits as we earnestly seek God. We sense that He is saying something. When we received salvation, we received the Holy Spirit, which is God's inner witness. God lives within us and is constantly speaking, but we must develop the ears to hear. When God speaks to us, He does it in a personal way based on our spiritual gifts. We need to make it a daily habit to simply take time to listen to Him, to ask Him to speak to us, and then to be still.

Connection to the word of God. Be diligent to study God's Word. Get serious about meditating on the Scriptures. These moments with God are more important than we think. The more we immerse ourselves in the Word, the more closely our thoughts, emotions, and decisions will align with what the spirit is saying to us, and the less power and strength other distractions and influences of the world will have on us. The word of God has given guidance in every matter under heaven since the beginning of time. If what we sense we are hearing contradicts the whole counsel or character of God as revealed in the Bible in any way, then it is not from God. God will not contradict himself. We must be in the moment with God. At times it may be that a Scriptural verse just grips us, and speaks directly and appropriately to a particular circumstance in our lives.

Communication with God. Constantly talk with God. We should take what we are hearing and ask God to show us clear direction and deeper revelation. Bring every issue to God and wait patiently and expectantly for Him to answer.

Counsel with people of wisdom. Seek the counsel of mature believers in Jesus Christ. We must ask God to provide us with godly, wise friends or mentors we can consult for counsel that we can trust, and maintain these relationships throughout life. See if their advice mirrors what we have been hearing from God's Word and from the Holy Spirit.

Confirmation of circumstances. God would use the circumstances of life, Scripture, and other believers to confirm His direction.

Consistency. God will continue to confirm His messages to us in ways only He could orchestrate, with shocking patterns of consistency.

*****

I will always remember the night God sent me a most amazing message and demonstrated His presence. I had cried myself to sleep that night and been sleeping for a couple of hours when I was awakened to the sound of music playing in the house. I opened my eyes waiting to see if it would stop and when it did not, I crept out of bed and followed the sound. Then I noticed a light coming from the computer in my office. My computer screen was lit up and Alvin Slaughter's song, "Sacrifice of Praise" was beaming from the computer. The lyrics, *"Lord I lift a song of worship, for Your glory and Your grace, let my heart reveal all my words fail to say, Lord receive this sacrifice of praise. On the mountain, in the valley, as I wait in my secret place, I will trust in the name of the Lord, now receive this sacrifice of praise,"* and it continued. Alvin Slaughter was proclaiming throughout the song, "Listen we declare today that some trust in horses, some trust in chariots, some trust in people, but we will trust in the name of the Lord!"

God had been teaching me through various ways about the power of praise in the midst of pain, but the anguish I felt was causing me to miss the message. The song playing on my computer in the middle of the night was God's consistency of again bringing it to my attention. I did begin to praise him and I felt the power of God come over me, but I also was filled with such curiosity, wondering how this was happening. I spoke out loud to God asking, "How is this happening?" when all of the sudden a fly landed on the start button on the left side of the screen of my computer, which lit up all of the programs. Then the fly rose and tapped on the programs button, then again on the music library folder, then again on the Alvin Slaughter album, and finally on the specific song. And somehow to do this the fly would have had to unlock the computer. Five different actions of the fly before the song played! The next song the fly played was "Lord I run to you," also by Alvin Slaughter. A burden lifted at that moment when I began to cry out and thank God for ministering to me. He knew I was desperate.

I cried out, "Thank you Lord, thank You. I need to hear from You. I need to know You are with me, and now You are showing me that again. I need your help Lord. I am desperate. Nobody will help me."

At that moment I heard the spirit of the Lord say, "I'll use a fly if I have to."

God reminded me in the most amazing way that He is with me always. For a person that had been feeling abandoned, His method was especially precious because of its uniqueness. I have never heard of other people experiencing God in this way.

God used a fly to serenade me while healing my heart and restoring my joy.

*****

I knew from that moment on that God was surely with me, but I still did not have answers to my prayers. What are God's answers to prayer? All of God's answers come through the lens of His perfect will. The more we understand what that perfect will is, the more we understand the answers, and the more we understand how and what we should seek. Often God responds with something that will prove to be far better than what we can even imagine. I believe it's really good to pray, "Lord would you do more than I can ask or imagine in this situation?"

Most of God's answers when you view them under the lighting of the Holy Spirit are variations of yes. I would describe them in four different types:

1. God answers *yes* immediately for two reasons. Firstly, when our request is aligned with God's will and timing He says *yes*. Secondly, He says *yes* immediately because He wants to give us a learning experience.
2. God says *yes* in due time. When God delays a request we should not automatically think the answer is *no*. Sometimes it is *yes*, but just not today. What He does give us today, if we will receive it, is the faith and patience to wait until the right time gets here.
3. God says *no* when the heart is not right. If motives for wanting something from God are wrong, then He wants to protect

us from harm that could result from the request.
4. God says *no* because He has a better plan. Often times our thinking is too limited because of our life experiences, and God wants something better for us.

What we must remember is just because our circumstances do not work out the way we want them to, and because we are faced with pain and suffering to walk out in this life, it does not mean that we do not hear from God. Our relationships with God are not simply in place to help us prevent the toils of this life, although sometimes they do. Our relationship with God is to help us to live out our lives in full purpose and destiny as God designed them to be. When not all makes sense, God will help us to find meaning.

The comfort we have as children of God that the rest of the world does not have is the great privilege of being able to personally talk with and speak into the ears of Almighty God. There is not an issue we face that prayer cannot address because nothing is too difficult or impossible for God to handle. It should not surprise us to discover that the greatest and most spiritually successful people in the Bible were always people of prayer. They modeled for us many different strategies that were documented for our use today.

Here we go.

> I will get through this because God is with me.
>
> My walk through fire may be painful,
>
> And it may be long,
>
> But with God's help I will overcome.
>
> In the meantime, I will be wise and hopeful because
>
> God will use IT for good.

SIX

Taunting Letters

After travailing in prayer for a long time, I started a bon fire to destroy every taunting paper that had a source of pain on it, and watched it burn.

-Dr. Lisa

King Hezekiah's life was a continual walk through fire, though he did have something good going for him. The key person of influence in his life was Isaiah. Isaiah was a mentor to King Hezekiah and his voice of reason, much like Paul was to Timothy.

We see a major leadership crisis in the life of Hezekiah in the Book of Isaiah, Chapter 37.

Control. Power plays. False narratives. Breeding fear. Destroying the lives of God's people. The people who know the truth do not speak because they are fearful. They are fearful of those in power over them and the harm that might come their way. Not much different from the modern day! For those in leadership of any kind are some moments of anguish when evil comes against them and tries to steal what they have done for the Glory of God. This is what happened to Hezekiah as described by Bishop T.D. Jakes, Senior Pastor of the Potter's House in Dallas, Texas, in his message, *Get Well Soon*.

Hezekiah's enemy was the Assyrian army, the terrorists of his day. The Assyrians had cut off water and food supplies, causing a destitute situation. Somehow, Hezekiah had to fix it. The Assyrians were trying to get Israel to turn against Hezekiah and against God by making both appear powerless in their eyes.

So Hezekiah followed in the footsteps of his forefather David, 10 generations back, and in those of his mentor Isaiah (certainly not in those of his father Ahaz, the idolater). Hezekiah drew himself to Isaiah, the man of God, and had the help of this prophet in seeking God.

In the meantime, the army tried to invoke fear and doubt in Hezekiah. They had the audacity to send him a threatening letter. And what did Hezekiah do? The scripture shows it best in 2 Kings 19:14-19:

¹⁴ After Hezekiah received the letter from the messengers and read it, he went up to the LORD's Temple and spread it out before the LORD. ¹⁵ And Hezekiah prayed this prayer before the LORD: "O LORD, God of Israel, you are enthroned between the mighty cherubim! You alone are God of all the kingdoms of the earth. You alone created the heavens and the earth. ¹⁶ Bend down, O LORD, and listen! Open your eyes, O LORD, and see! Listen to Sennacherib's words of defiance against the living God. ¹⁷ "It is true, LORD, that the kings of Assyria have destroyed all these nations. ¹⁸ And they have thrown the gods of these nations into the fire and burned them. But of course the Assyrians could destroy them! They were not gods at all—only idols of wood and stone shaped by human hands. ¹⁹ Now, O LORD our God, rescue us from his

power; then all the kingdoms of the earth will know that you alone, O LORD, are God." (NLT)

What sorts of taunting letters or documents have we received that need to be spread out before the Lord? What did Hezekiah do that we can learn from? He completely turned everything over to God because he knew he had no control and that he needed God's help. There is another thing that goes along with Hezekiah's need. Hezekiah was confident about bringing the matter before the Lord. Even though he was in a desperate situation and he was likely scared to death, he did what he knew to do. He took the matter straight to the Lord and awaited an answer and this is what God did after a series of events recorded in 2 Kings 19:35:

35 "That night the angel of the LORD went out to the Assyrian camp and killed 185,000 Assyrian soldiers. When the surviving Assyrians woke up the next morning, they found corpses everywhere." (NLT)

Imagine that! Imagine God literally destroying our enemies by sending an angel to fight for us. From this passage we know that one angel of the Lord is powerful enough to destroy at least 185,000 people at a time.

One thing the Scripture tells us that should be comforting to know is that God gives angels charge over us. History tells us that God has the ability to come to our rescue, and that He will come when it is according to His will.

*****

Thoughts of taunting letters bring to mind instant negative thoughts and frustration. Then overwhelming feelings of anger set in. We must deal with it. We must let go of the anger and frustration.

I decided to create a physical representation of releasing all of the taunting things. I gathered up all the documents or physical things that represent what has come against me and laid them out before God and cried out to

Him. After travailing in prayer for a long time, I started a bon fire and destroyed every taunting paper with a source of pain on it, and watched it burn.

One of my secret weapons that helped me through this process was various worship songs like "I'm Going to Lay it Down," by Jaci Valasquez, a song I would play over and over. If near a computer, look it up and play it now.

After hours of sobbing and crying out to God, so much that my throat was raw, I set a big bon fire in the pit in my back yard and DECIDED to walk it out until I could testify to these words in the song:

I'm gonna lay it down, I'm gonna learn to trust You now, What else can I do everything I am depends on You, and if the sun don't come back up, Your love will be enough, I'm gonna let it be, I'm gonna let it go, I'm gonna lay it down.

It took a very long time and it was very painful, but at that moment I wrote my Overcomer's creed, adapted from the creed in Max Lucado's series, *You'll Get Through This* and I posted it in every room of my house.

Get ready! Get ready! Get ready!

> I will get through this because God is with me.
>
> My walk through fire may be painful,
>
> And it may be long,
>
> But with God's help I will overcome.
>
> In the meantime, I will be wise and hopeful because
>
> God will use IT for good.

SEVEN

Bad News from God

The struggle to recover is more intense than the struggle of affliction. We have to work to recover, which is what nobody tells us and it is all uphill. Faith without works does not work.

- Dr. Lisa

Over the years, Hezekiah had done much to reestablish order and worship in the tumultuous times that followed the reign of his father. Then things went wrong.

Why, we wonder, do bad things happen to good people?

Hezekiah's father was an idolater who had corrupted Judea with his ways. Hezekiah, on the other hand, was the extreme opposite of his father. Hezekiah ruled as king of Judah at the same time his father did because they were co-regents, yet they operated very differently from one another. Hezekiah was dedicated to God, fought against idolatry, and was able to bring true worship and holiness back to the people. He was a good person, even though his environment and parenting could have easily led him to follow in his father's evil footsteps. If his father had been the one getting sick, we could understand, but when we have done well and we reap badly anyway, our experience is painful.

Does anybody understand what it is like to be shortchanged?

I can relate to Hezekiah because he was a warrior – a man of results. He measured his effectiveness for God through his accomplishments. He was meant to fight. He was not meant to lie in a sick bed.

There is nothing tougher than being built for battle yet having to lie sick. This man had ridden horses, commanded chariots, and subdued armies. He had run into villages filled with fire and fought his way out and suddenly he was lying in the bed and wondering how he ended up like that.

Imagine the demonic voices speaking to Hezekiah: "Where is your God now?" Hezekiah was likely taunted by the Devil who told him, "You might as well have left those idols up. You built back the temple but what good does it do you now?"

I have heard those same voices. We all hear them.

What do we do when it seems like faith doesn't work? What do we do when we have prayed for other people and they were blessed, yet when we prayed for our own situations, they got worse? What do we do when we can help everybody but ourselves? What do we do when we know we are fighters who have fallen off our horses and now we are lying on our backs?

There is no captivity like the captivity a warrior goes through when confined. There are many different ways to be confined but Hezekiah was confined to bed.

These are the things that try our souls.

These are the situations that challenge our faith.

These are the conditions the Bible describes as the opportune time of the enemy.

We all have to live between two voices. One is telling us to do right and the other is telling us to do wrong. One is taunting us saying, "Where is your faith?" And the other is saying, "Hold on to God."

*****

Is it not strange how faith and fear can abide in the same place at the same time?

T.D. Jakes describes the situation in Hezekiah's life in his message, *Get Well Soon*. When Hezekiah received a visit from Isaiah, he was happy because Hezekiah loved Isaiah and had assumed he had good news. But that time, Isaiah delivered the kind of news that knocks the wind out of a person.

In those days Hezekiah [king of Judah] became sick and was at the point of death. Isaiah the prophet, the son of Amoz, came to him and said, "For the LORD says this, 'Set your house in order *and* prepare a will, for you shall die; you will not live.'"² Then Hezekiah turned his face to the wall and prayed to the LORD,³ and said, "Please, O LORD, just remember how I have walked before You in faithfulness *and* truth, and with a whole heart [absolutely devoted to You], and have done what is good in Your sight." And Hezekiah wept greatly. (Isaiah 38:1-3 AMP)

Isaiah walked in the house and told Hezekiah God said to "Put your house in order, for surely you are going to die and you will not recover."

Now the general person would doubt what was said or minimize it in some way, but not in this situation. Isaiah was known as the eagle eye prophet, clear and precise.

Precise like an eagle, so there was no doubt about this prophecy being the will of God.

Isaiah was the very embodiment of everything Hezekiah understood about God, and he told Hezekiah that he would not recover from his sickness. Isaiah had spoken, "You will die."

And then Hezekiah began to struggle.

The struggle to recover is more intense than the struggle of affliction. We have to work to recover, which is what nobody tells us and it is all uphill. Faith without works does not work.

We struggle with the enemy as he does everything to convince us he can deny us the promises of God.

We reject his denial and choose to believe God no matter what.

We struggle to trust God and His promises while we are distrusting of our own thoughts and feelings.

We struggle to keep our hearts tender in the presence of God.

We struggle with the belief that the promises of God are more than just words of comfort, but rather part of a higher vision God has to give us of abundant life.

We have felt like every meal was our last supper before our arrest, our trial, and our crucifixion, and we were not even sure there was going to be a resurrection.

Yes, we have to work out our faith. We have to decide that we will be partakers of the nature of Christ himself. We have to take on His attributes. We have to walk in peace, love, and joy regardless of the circumstances.

He IS more than a conqueror and He HAS overcome every single attack of the enemy and things of the world. We have to be determined to do the same.

So with all of these thoughts and feelings Hezekiah had reeling around, he had some work to do. He told God, I've got a good résumé. Look at my résumé. Look at my background. Look at how I tried to serve you. Look at how I tried to worship you. Look how I tore down all the idols and restored your temple. I fought for you, stood up for you, and you put my life at risk!

What do we do when we have been fighters and we fall off our horses?

We cannot let the pain that we are going through deter the purpose that God has for our lives.

In all of Hezekiah's desperation, he did something unusual. He took the case of praise before God, and all of a sudden God changed His verdict.

Bishop Jakes points out that we can notice something interesting related to Hezekiah's writing in Isaiah 38:10-20 that we do not see in 2 Kings. When Hezekiah recovered from his illness, he recorded his prayer to the Lord.

Not only did God answer his prayer favorably but He gave Hezekiah a sign that He was going to help him. He told Hezekiah ahead of time, restoring protection and solving the mystery. God basically said, "Hezekiah if you're going to praise me, I'll add 15 years to your life."

It seemed like it was over for Hezekiah. Isaiah was on his way out. Surely he heard from God, but just before he could get out of the outer court, the word of the Lord came to Isaiah, and all of the sudden, God reported to Isaiah that He had reversed the decision. How did this happen?

In this situation, the only thing we can understand is that Hezekiah was tied into a higher law of the universe, one of God's laws, like the law of gravity against the law of aerodynamics. There is a higher law that supersedes the lower ones. The lower laws say, "If you are sick, you will die." But the higher law says, "If you praise God, He will bring you out."

*****

There are many universal laws that exist but they are God's laws. The universe simply obeys the laws God has put in place. Even though God did not bring me out the way I wanted Him to God has assured me nothing is going to stop the destiny he has placed within me.

Last year my friend Tanya had given me a Hyacinth flower and I planted it in my yard just outside my back door so I could see it bloom just as I stepped onto the deck. Several months passed and I forgot the exact place I planted it and made the mistake of putting a large round stepping stone on top of it. It is spring time now and I noticed the flower had stretched forth from under the rock making a beautiful lavender blue bloom. At that moment I heard the spirit of the Lord say, "Nothing is going to stop what I have planted within you!" Praise God!

I moved the rock off the top of the flower and noticed the stems were light green and flattened to the ground due to the weight of the stone. But the next day, after the weight had been removed the stems and all parts of the flower was springing forth and darkening. The entire plant was beginning to bloom as it was intended.

I discovered the meaning of the lavender blue hyacinth flower is constancy. Constancy is defined as being faithful, dependable, enduring and unchanging, all qualities of God.

I thank God for serenading me with the fly. I thank God for the brothers and sisters in Christ that have warred for me when I needed it most. And I thank God for putting a flower at my back door to remind me of His faithfulness and how nothing, absolutely nothing, no matter how much it may weigh me down, will stop the purpose God has put in place for my life.

*****

My friend Dan Harris can truly be considered a modern day Hezekiah. Dan was in one hospital in the midst of serious heart failure when his doctor told him that he would have to immediately be air lifted by helicopter to another hospital and undergo heart surgery. Otherwise, he would die, and there was a risk that the surgery would not work. While being airlifted to a hospital in Lexington, Kentucky, he, like Hezekiah, appealed to God.

Out loud in that helicopter with a Christian nurse sitting next to him, Dan told God he was ready to go, but his family was not. He asked God to extend his life so that he could make sure his family would be well taken care of. He told God he would retire from work and begin working for Him full time. He promised God he would teach the Gospel if God would let him live another 17 years. He knew his gift of teaching was needed in the body of Christ, so he promised God he would teach his Word if He would extend Dan's life.

God granted Dan his wish. His health problems were completely reversed, and he is now in the eighteenth year since his heart complications. He has great all around health. Dan has authored two books, and teaches the adult Bible class every week in our church, and sometimes co-teaches the Bible Scholars class with me. God has blessed Dan not only with good health but also with a purposeful, abundant life. The higher law came into effect for Dan as well. What causes a higher law to come into effect?

As people of God, we know the power of prayer, and at our lowest times we may not be able to form the words to speak.

What do we do when we see no evidence of God's intervention?

Do we not have enough faith?

Do we not believe God enough?

Are we not praying the right prayers?

When we have done all we can, we just need to focus on grace. Sometimes the deepness of our wounded hearts will not allow us to do so. So, that is the time we need other prayer warriors.

Here is a good prayer borrowed from Bishop Jakes' message in a time like this:

Father, I thank you because you have the grace that is sufficient enough to heal, to deliver, to strengthen, and to fortify. When healing is delayed, your Grace is still sufficient. Give that grace to those who are praying with me right now that whatever state they are in, they can look to you as the author and the finisher of their faith in Jesus name. Amen.

Ready?

I will get through this because God is with me.

My walk through fire may be painful,

And it may be long,

But with God's help I will overcome.

In the meantime, I will be wise and hopeful because

God will use IT for good.

EIGHT

Stairway to Fear

"Peace is not the absence of trouble. Peace is the presence of God in the trouble."

- Dr. Lisa

On a freezing cold January day, after years of battling the *IT* regarding the legal issues related to the school, I stood before a judge for finality on the matter. God sent me legal counsel Clyde Bennett and Anthony Vannoy to come to my rescue when my previous legal counsel for the case had withdrawn right on the day we were set for trial after having drained all of my resources. Thus, I was manipulated into a plea deal. (That is a story in itself, but needless to say, we should never trust people with our well being who have already shown us they cannot be trusted.)

My new legal counsel tried to reverse the terrible misrepresentation I was given up until this point, but on this day it was to no avail. I had been sentenced to 120 days incarceration in an annex to the county jail called the Talbert House and had to pay $75,000 restitution.

My aunt told everyone I was sentenced to the same place they sent Pete Rose after he had been convicted of gambling on baseball. The place may have had the same name, but this certainly was not that place. I had been sentenced to a place that I used to go to visit the parents of my students when they were incarcerated to see how they were doing and to give them updates about their children. The visits to that place were bad enough, and now I was going to be incarcerated there myself.

I loved my students and my staff, and am thankful for the miracles of God in that community, but was building a school in the inner city worth all of this?

I stood devastated by having been deceived by the previous legal counsel, and now my new attorney was not able to yet correct it and I was going to be incarcerated. After having been fingerprinted, photographed, x-rayed and all the other processing they do when a person is under community control, I was taken into what they call the hole and left there in the freezing cold with no shoes and a small thin blanket. I told the corrections officer I was not supposed to be in there, but the response was to shove what resembled a bologna sandwich in a bag in my hands and to say, "Well, you're going to be here now."

I was terrified as I walked into the cell. I set the bologna sandwich down on a metal shelf that hung on a wall. There was a dirty silver metal toilet and sink, and a metal bed attached to the wall with the thin green mat on it. The room smelled of urine. There was a window about four inches high and 10 inches wide that went across the back of the cell where piercing cold air poured in, but the view was even more excruciating.

The only view was of the offices of the person who had used the injustice on my life as an opportunity for advancement of his. Every evil thing that was attempted on my life seemed to hit me spot on.

At the start of this cold January day, I believed all of my legal issues and the injustice on my life was about to be over. I thought the judge would have better discernment and rule in my favor, but that was not the case. Something had gone on behind the scenes with the previous attorney that lengthened my tribulation. I thought that God was going to come to my rescue with some mighty act, but He did not and I felt a deep sense of abandonment. My real problems had just begun. The last four years were simply a foreshadowing of what was to come. Exhausted from the fight, I was engulfed in worry, anxiety, and fear knowing from that day forward my life would never be the same.

*****

Worry, anxiety, and fear are really the same thing emotionally. They are just experienced on different levels. They are stair steps. Worry step one, anxiety is the next level up, and then fear the highest level.

Fear is a negative emotion caused by a real or perceived threat to our well-being. Anxiety is also experienced in different intensities. Anxiety is to be uneasy and nervous about an event, person, or problem we cannot control. We are anxious because we cannot control *IT*. We wish we could, but we cannot, so we feel anxious about it. Worry is to mentally dwell on difficulty or trouble. *IT* is simply a chronic concern. Worry is the lowest level, but it can turn into anxiety and fear. Fear can subside to anxiety and worry. So it is really the same emotion. It is just experienced on different levels. Yet we are commanded in Scripture not to do any of the three.

We are commanded in scripture not to fear, not to be anxious, and not to worry. God would never command us not to do something if we could not. Right?

So God has commanded us not to fear. "Do not fear" or "fear not" are the most common commandments in the Bible. I was intrigued to find out that God mentions fear 365 times. Is this because he knew we needed 365 reminders for each day of the year? Hmm... Regardless, God created us to live in peace, not in fear.

*****

Last fall I was able to go to Israel with Pastor Tommy Bates and a group of about 40 people. We were able to walk and see biblical historical sites where Jesus walked and we were able to see places where He prayed. It was a magnificent trip.

It was amazing to be at the place where Jesus was, but there was something that stood out. Every time we met a Jewish person, we would greet him or her with the word "shalom." I love the word shalom. This Hebrew word is very significant. It means peace.

Who does not want to have peace? Who does not want to live in tranquility free from strife in a great atmosphere? But the truth of the matter is as long as we live on this physical earth, there will always be something trying to steal our peace. There will be something trying to take that shalom.

The Bible says that we are to seek peace, which tells us that the object of peace is very important. It tells us a lot of things in life. It's something we have to go after. We have to seek it and we have to maintain it. We have to stay with it and pursue it and not let it get out of our sight.

Peace is not the absence of trouble. Peace is the presence of God in the trouble. It is a constant of God's presence in our lives. God gives us peace as a gift if we have been justified by faith. We are a friend of God. We have to pursue it. We have to have peace with ourselves. We have to have peace with other people and our circumstances. It is not what is going on. It is about the constant presence of God.

It was the night before Jesus was going to be crucified. It was the night before He was going to be arrested, beaten and bruised, when He said, "I give you peace, not as the world gives." He said, "Do not let your heart be troubled; I have overcome the world." He was not saying I have great peace because I am not going to go through anything. He was saying, "I have great peace regardless of what I am about to go through because I know I am going to come through the other side victorious."

God wants to give us this peace that is going to get us through to the other side. Undamaged. It's not a matter of not going through something. It is a matter of having peace in the midst of our walk through fire.

*****

As much as we know the presence of God by peace, we know the presence of the devil by fear.

God never created us to live in fear. That is why through the Bible we are constantly commanded not to fear, for God does not want us to live that way. In Philippians 4:6, Paul says, "Be anxious for nothing..." (NKJV)

Yes, the Bible tells us to be anxious for not one thing. We have the ability to live without anxiety. Anxiety and stress on any level are the number one reason for sickness and disease in America, the number one reason for prescribed medications, the number one reason for visits to the doctor. Stress and anxiety are killers on every level. They literally cause our life span to decrease.

What about worry? Jesus said, "Therefore I say to you, do not worry about your life, what you will eat, or what you will drink, nor about your body, what you will put on..." (Matthew 6:25 NKJV)

By the way, Jesus also told us we were not to worry about tomorrow because tomorrow has enough problems of its own. He would never say that if we did not have the ability to eliminate worry.

The problem is that a prolonged walk through fire can breed worry, anxiety, and fear. It can cause emotional problems that can lead to physical ones.

Some of us fear people, some fear failure, some fear rejection, and some fear financial problems. People can have anxiety regarding just about anything.

When fears are operating in our lives, they can cause us to have relational problems and emotional problems. Fears can cause us to be distracted parents, have poor performance in the workplace, and destroy just about anything in our lives.

Remember I told you that I thought God had abandoned me? I had lost confidence in God because I felt if He loved me, He would protect me from harm. Up until this point, every target against me had hit me spot on. The intense level of worry, anxiety, and fear that surrounded me was more than any person can take.

Well, the root of all worry, anxiety, and fear comes from not having confidence in our Heavenly Father. This is what is known as an orphan spirit as described in a sermon given by Kerry Shook, Senior Pastor of Woodlands Church. What we know about

God is that He loves to be a daddy. In the context of Jesus' statement, not worrying is the context of God being our Father.

The reason so many of us grow up with worry, anxiety, and fear is that many of us never had a father, so we do not know there is somebody taking care of us.

World renowned Christian communicator Joyce Meyer has shared a testimony about her prolonged walk through fire throughout childhood. Her earthly father had raped her over 200 times. She was abused from the time she was a young girl for 12-15 years until she left home at age 18. Talk about not being able to trust one's father! Her mom did nothing about it and she spent many lonely years. Because of this trauma, I imagine it may have been hard for her to have complete trust in her Heavenly Father. Over a period of time God was able to heal her wounds and allow her to use it to minister to millions all over the world, many that have had to live in similar anguish. The evil that came against Joyce in her life is now used for good and somehow God worked it out for His glory, did He not? God gifted her to help people but the enemy hoped all she would do is hurt people. Too bad devil. God wins this one.

As I was growing up, I did have a wonderful earthly father but still did not have the right concept of how much God loves His fatherly role. This realization came as a result of prayers that I felt were unanswered and from my disappointment with God allowing the wicked to prosper. I resented Him for the prolonged pain that I felt He permitted in my life.

What I should have done was cling to God, but at the time I allowed my suffering to distance my heart from Him.

Most parents say their children and grandchildren are their greatest joys in life and when they need something it brings sorrow if they do not ask. This is God's heart toward us. He knows everything about us. He knows the number of hairs on our heads. And in every circumstance, He loves to be our Abba Father, our Daddy.

The root issue of all fear, anxiety, and worry is an orphan spirit. How many times has the joy in our life been robbed by worry, anxiety, and fear? How much have we lost at the expense of those we love the most?

God has shown us how we are going to overcome these three things. God says, focus on Me.

We need to consider worry and anxiety as enemies of our lives. We deal with this every day, especially at the beginning of the day.

The love, joy, and peace of God are normal. Worry, anxiety, and fear are not normal. The reason that worry exists so often is that we become so familiar with it that we just think it is a normal part of life.

Worry is robbing us of God. It is robbing us of joy.

We are in complete control of these three areas. God would never command us to do something that we do not have the ability to do. God tells us, "Do not be anxious."

Consider worry, anxiety, and fear as agents of the enemy to destroy our lives and to rob us of joy. This means that the devil has implanted something in our lives and *IT* is just sitting there intimidating us. Because of that, we cannot focus on God and the people that we love.

These three negative emotions rob us of our ability to worship God and to love the people that we love, so they are the enemy.

Turn every anxious and worrisome thought into a prayer until victory comes!

Again, Philippians 4:6-7 says, "Be anxious for nothing, but in everything by prayer and supplication, with thanksgiving, let your requests be made known to God; and the peace of God, which surpasses all understanding, will guard your hearts and minds through Christ Jesus." (NKJV)

*****

When we wake up in the morning we should not always have a planned out prayer list. Rather, we should have a list that says this is what is bothering us today. Have we ever tried to pray yet our minds wandered? What we really ought to be praying about is what comes on our mind. We are trying to pray but we are thinking about that guy we hate to have a meeting with. Our minds are wandering and these anxious thoughts come into our minds. While we are trying to pray for something, we will either pray or we will worry. Our old worry list becomes our new prayer list. All day long, rather than being able to enjoy our lives and the people in our lives, we are just focused on the liability, the potential harms that can come from the situation today or sometime in the future, and that is the problem.

Supplication means anything that helps us pray more effectively: fasting, reading the word, worship, anything that helps us in our prayers.

What does it mean when we say with thanksgiving let our requests be made known unto God? This means that when I am praying I am thankful that He loves me, He is hearing me, and He is going to answer my prayers.

Jesus said, Father I thank You that You hear my prayers. Thank You, Father. I'm coming to You because You know everything going on my life and You care about it and I'm thanking You right now that you're hearing this prayer and that You will answer me from heaven.

We walk through the day all day long not worrying about whether God can do it. We are thanking God because we know He is the best Father in the Universe.

Well-fathered children are fearless children.

Pastor Shook describes it best when he says, "The root of all fear and anxiety is an orphaned spirit because orphans are on their own and they have to take care of their own problems. And the devil wants you to feel as though you are on your own and you have to solve your own problems."

*****

While I was incarcerated, I believe nearly 100% of the women I encountered had an orphaned spirit.

The worst part for me in that environment had to be the violence, profanities, and obscenities I heard around the clock. There was no escape. The F-word was used for every purpose under the sun. Some people could not use a sentence without it. All 50 women on the second floor were stuck together in one large room and every conversation contained either the F-word or the MF-word. The F-word was used as a noun, a verb, an adjective, an adverb, and just any other form of speech, even if there was no purpose for it.

After I was at the jail for a while, the inmates began to treat me with respect. They referred to me as Miss Lisa. Although there were no Bibles there (and you could only order a Quran through the commissary) somehow a Catholic Bible was left in the locker next to my bed from a previous inmate. I constantly read it and prayed whenever I could, even though there was no privacy. When inmates had court dates to appear before judges, many would ask me to help them write letters of remorse to their judges and many would ask me to pray with them.

Once I gained respect with the inmates, when they would use profanities or obscenities, they would cover their mouths in embarrassment and apologize or say "excuse me." The environment had improved a great deal, and I believe it was because there was a better jail culture, if you will. Some of the inmates with more aggressive behavior had moved on to other jails or had been let out so those on the floor now were classified as minimum risk. Instead of sitting around with idle time, everyone began to have healthy communication, watch positive television shows and movies, and began play cards, Scrabble, and other games.

Some days I was able to teach small group Bible studies with the women. The topics we did I would never do in a church environment. I would start with a few and some days I would look up and there would be a whole herd. To draw the interest of the women, I would pick passages that were most shocking and relatable to them and then pose a question for discussion. The women loved the love stories like Hosea and Song of Solomon but the most memorable was the study from Judges 19. Here there were reprobates that approached a home for sexual favors where men of God were staying. This ended up with a dead concubine that had been chopped up in 12 pieces. The parts of the corpse were delivered to every territory in Israel. There was an intense discussion that day when the question posed from the scripture was, "How could this have happened?"

There are many stories in the Bible like this I never learned in Sunday school that certainly came in handy during this time. I think God had these stories in there for such a time as this and to let us know how depraved the world really has become.

One woman in particular had decided that she was going to turn her life around. She was no longer going to do drugs, and she was going to go to a program after jail for six months to get completely clean and to get back on track in her life. She was so proud of how she was going to reform because she felt she had a strong support system.

Now my support system was my family and friends from my church, specifically my brother who is also a psychologist, and my closest friends who are mostly ministers. When I found out who her support system was, I realized how seriously in trouble our society is.

I will call this young woman Mindy for now. She was so thrilled because her sugar daddy, the older gentleman that supported her and with whom she was in the sexual relationship, was going to take care of her financially. She had met the man while she was prostituting. He promised her when she got out of jail this time that the two of them would go on a cruise.

Now keep in mind this gentleman was not Mindy's boyfriend. Her boyfriend was someone else who was also incarcerated. When he got out, she said he also wanted her to stay clean. Her boyfriend was also her "dope boy" who supplied her with drugs. Her mother was the one who got her on the drugs and taught her how to prostitute. As a matter of fact, the woman, her mother, forced Mindy to sell her body. Her mother would stand on one corner and Mindy would stand on the other, and they would do what is known as working the block together. That was how they survived. Her mother had been clean for a while, and so Mindy believed she could stay clean as well.

I pray that God send strong Christian men and women into Mindy's life to minister to her and to break the chains the enemy has on her life. I did my best to try to help her and the other women while I was there, but

I do not know how effective I was. I was experiencing my own trauma, but I did try to put it aside enough to help those that I could.

A woman there, my age, now clean from heroin addiction, had become a friend of mine while we were incarcerated. Amy taught me all about street life and jail culture because she was concerned about my survival in the environment. Now thanks to Amy I have a whole new vocabulary that I am certain I would never have known without her. She and I must have played 100 games of Scrabble. Can you imagine the different kinds of words we might have had on that board? It was rare that Amy beat me, but when she did you might have thought she had conquered Mount Everest.

During these days, I was able to impact Amy's life but she impacted mine too. I believe in some odd way God used her to minister to me. She was no doubt instrumental in the healing of my soul. We would station ourselves on a small couch against the wall in the middle of the room so we could see both entrances and monitor the activities, partly for the safety factor and partly for the humor factor. At times we would see fists thrown and blood flying and at times we roared in laughter. There were regular outrageous antics that took place that one cannot imagine that even my decades of serving in the inner city could not have prepared me.

About midway through the time I was incarcerated, something remarkable happened. One of my students from the school showed up as a fellow inmate. Now superintendent and student were incarcerated in the exact same place, in the exact same dorm room. I knew immediately when (I will call her) Sadie came in the room that she had been my student. Sadie came over to where Amy and I were playing scrabble and said, "Hi Miss Hamm, how you doing?" We hugged one another tightly and then sat down to talk. It was hard for us to have a private conversation because every inmate in the room was staring at us by then. Everyone already knew my story because we were forced to share why we were there in group.

Once a few people knew, everybody did. Sadie knew why I was there already because her siblings were still at the school. She was informed by her mom that I might be there, but I gave it my best shot to explain it to her anyway. Really, how do you explain such a thing to a young person? What we were doing at the school was not just giving a quality education, but giving students a chance to see the good things in life that they could reach for instead of continuing to live in cycles of dysfunction.

I wanted to prevent the one-in-three black males and one-in-six black females who would be incarcerated, and I wanted them to be the positive contributors to society. I wanted to prevent all of the educators that start out and education and leave the field very soon after entering because the challenges are too great and because they do not have adequate support. Only now, that vision reversed on me and I was now incarcerated and I was not out of education.

I was in a place I was never supposed to be. My mantra to the students was always that if you get an education, work hard and commit your life to God, your life would be different than those who live with the norm of poverty, violence, incarceration, and murder. How could I still give Sadie hope that working hard, getting an education, and being committed to God would equate to success when my life was no longer an example of it?

Essentially, I told her that the auditors who work for the state of Ohio determined money spent at the school for student and staff incentives was a criminal act and I was charged for it. This was confusing to her as it was to everyone. Adding value to people is a good thing but apparently to the state auditors it was so rare for them to see this they deemed it criminal. But we know the Bible tells us, in the last days what is good will be called bad, and what is bad will be called good (Isaiah 5:20; 2 Timothy 3.)

Sadie had seen on the news how I had been accused of misspending because I had taken 20 girls to a Justin Bieber concert and a different group to a Taylor Swift concert. She knew because her sister was one of the girls. Sadie felt bad about what had happened and said everyone was asking how I could get in trouble for spending money on students at my own school with the money we raised ourselves.

I explained that sometimes people who are in government agencies think they know better than the people who actually run the schools, and they end up making mistakes that hurt people, and this is one of those examples. I explained to her that sometimes when I would take the teachers and the principals to a conference, we would go out to a restaurant or to the theater or a sporting event and the state auditors did not like the way that money was spent, so they called such events a type of theft. That explanation was more than enough for her.

Sadie did love God, but like most of the children at the school, she had an orphan spirit. But one thing I can be thankful for, even though my legacy of the school itself was taken away from me, the legacy of the love of God that was implanted in all of the students can never be taken away. There is no question that every person was introduced to God and experienced His love while having been a part of what I now refer to as my mission.

*****

God is the best Father in the Universe. Rejoice in this. He is our Father and He loves us. He loves helping us process anything in our lives. Nothing is too small. Nothing is too large. He just enjoys the relationship. If we are obsessing about something, it means that we are wasting the relationship we have with God.

We know we have prayed enough when we have peace. The saints of old called this "praying through." Pastor Tommy Bates of Community Family Church in Independence, Kentucky has a ministry called "Bridging the Gap." His ministry is on television with the intention of informing the body of Christ about the travailing of God and the perseverance the saints had in what he calls the "Old Time Way." What is meant by praying through is to pray until we get that peace.

My spiritual mother and mentor Pastor Darlene Bishop of Solid Rock Church experienced bleeding in her breasts. She would weep before God as she washed the blood out of her gown. I can remember her testifying time and time again about eight women who stayed days with her praying through until she was healed.

The Word says peace will guard our hearts and our minds, our thoughts and our feelings. The word *guard* in the original Greek actually means to guard against a military invasion. When we are at peace, we may not understand why we have so much peace. We should envision this concept as a military guard around our hearts and our minds so the devil cannot penetrate us with fear, anxiety, and worry.

We need to make this practical, not religious or spiritual. We must put our eyes on God and enjoy our lives by faith knowing that our Father is in control.

We are not orphans but well-fathered people in the world. All we have got to do is believe that and have confidence in it. For some of us, the circumstances make believing this truth very challenging, but remember Jesus said in Matthew 6:31-32, your Heavenly Father knows that you need all things. He wants to attend and father you through your life. He's the answer to every problem.

I felt God had abandoned me, but the truth is He was with me every step of the way.

Over an extended period, people in the body of Christ surrounded me like a herd of buffalo protecting their young from a ferocious lion. I had become paralyzed with fear. They recognized the attack of the enemy on my life and they began surrounding me so closely so that while I was bleeding, animals smelling blood for another attack could not touch me.

The truth is God sent them. He sent them to help me overcome, and every time I say the Overcomer's creed I am reminded of his various acts of mercy, kindness and grace.

Shout it out!

I will get through this because God is with me.

My walk through fire may be painful,

And it may be long,

But with God's help I will overcome.

In the meantime, I will be wise and hopeful because

God will use IT for good.

*For more on experiences while incarcerated and unexpected friendship see the *Walking Through Fire* Bible Study Series.

NINE

Paralyzed

I knew if I didn't leave any bitterness, hatred, or unforgiveness behind, I would remain in a state of paralysis.

-Dr. Lisa

Nikki and Pablo had been fighting over something they should never been concerned about. The secret they were keeping from each other had created a wedge between them that had bred serious feelings of mistrust for one another. When the lies were uncovered, things went from bad to worse. It was bad enough to begin with when their crashed plane had left them stranded on an island with a group of people. Still, what they were focusing on at the moment was a bag of useless jewels they kept hidden from one another. This was the storyline in the popular television series *Lost*. Even though I knew this story line was fiction, the thought of this shook me to my core.

Through a series of events, both Nikki and Pablo were bitten by a poisonous spider that left them paralyzed for hours to the point they appeared dead. They had no detectable heartbeat. The other survivors on the island did not know what happened to the couple, but they laid their bodies next to each other on the beach and stared at them helplessly.

Now on this island was a doctor and a scientist, but the people who spotted Nikki and Pablo decided to make a fatal decision without any inquiry of these experts. The two appeared to be dead, so the survivors began digging their graves. Nikki and Pablo were neither moving nor breathing, or so it appeared. So, in a very short period of time they were buried alive. The closing scene shows a shovel full of dirt falling on the face of Nikki as her eyes open. She could not speak or move, but in the final moments she was able to open her eyes. Nobody was paying attention. Nobody saw her because they were too busy with the task of covering her in dirt to finish the burial. The story does not end well.

Let us contemplate this. How often do we see this in the world? How often do we see this in the body of Christ? Now, we may not physically bury people alive, but we do bury them in other ways. We dismiss them, distance ourselves from them, abandon them, or write them off like a politician running for office who no longer wants to be associated with someone they feel may tarnish their reputation. Someone's heart is in anguish and we do not give them the time of day. Someone suddenly becomes an inconvenience because they can no longer be a resource to us in their time of pain. Actions like this become ways to bury others. We become tools of the enemy instead of vessels of salt and light.

The enemy comes only to steal, and to kill, and to destroy, but Jesus said, "I have come that they might have life and have it more abundantly." (John 10:10, NKJV)

We are children of God. We do not bury things. We resurrect them!

*****

I read an article in which the author described his experience of being paralyzed. He said at first he asked, "Why me?" but over time just "Why live? He described the determination to suppress feelings of rage and how he had to balance acceptance and the desire to surrender. Everything was in a state of uncooperativeness for him, and he began to understand that he could not have desires. To have those desires just made him realize there were many things he could not have. Everything in life was forever changed. He could no longer enjoy the simple pleasures in life like reading a book in solitude because somebody else had to turn the pages.

There is physical paralysis, and then there is paralysis of the soul and the spirit. It may be brought on by physical illness or emotional trauma, the various uses of drugs or medication, alcohol abuse, or a combination of various circumstances. Life can deal some pretty hard blows that can lead to a spiraling down effect:

- A horrendous accident like the father who finds he has run over his 4-year-old son and killed him when the boy only meant to welcome his dad home.
- The news of a loved one who has committed suicide.
- The community that has been devastated by a natural disaster.

What do we do when something of this magnitude happens?

All of us have times of paralysis. One of the greatest people of faith that we know in recent days, Mother Teresa, demonstrated this point when she said, "The place of God in my soul is blank. There is no God in me. When the pain of longing is so great—I just long & long for God... and then it is that I feel He does not want me—He is not there—God does not want me."

Mark Mallett, a Roman Catholic singer/songwriter and missionary writes on his web site, *The Now Word,* "For the times trials are so intense, temptations so fierce, emotions so embroiled, the mind is spinning; I want to rest, but my body is reeling; I want to believe, but my soul is wrestling with a thousand doubts. Sometimes, these are moments of *spiritual warfare*—an attack by the enemy to discourage and drive the soul into sin and despair... but permitted nonetheless by God to allow the soul to see its weakness and constant need for Him, and thus draw nearer to the Source of its strength."

Mark 2:1-6,11-12 describes a man who was paralyzed body, mind, and soul but he had four friends determined to do whatever it took to get him to Jesus – the answer.

¹ Jesus returned to Capernaum, and a few days later the news went out that He was at home. ² So many people gathered together that there was no longer room [for them], not even near the door; and Jesus was discussing with them the word [of God]. ³ Then they came, bringing to Him a paralyzed

man, who was being carried by four men. ⁴When they were unable to get to Him because of the crowd, they [a]removed the roof above Jesus; and when they had dug out an opening, they let down the mat on which the paralyzed man was lying. ⁵When Jesus saw their [active] faith [springing from confidence in Him], He said to the paralyzed man, "Son, your sins are forgiven." ... ¹¹ "I say to you, get up, pick up your mat and go home." ¹² And he got up and immediately picked up the mat and went out before them all, so that they all were astonished and they glorified *and* praised God, saying, "We have never seen anything like this!" (AMP)

In this parable of the paralytic, the ill man says nothing. We can assume he wants to be healed, but he of course had no power to even bring himself to Christ's feet. It was his *friends* who brought him to Jesus.

The season of my personal walk through fire in which I experienced the death of my father, extensive legal battles resulting from false accusations, and the loss of my freedom was so horrific and prolonged that my soul became paralyzed.

What made it worse was that nearly all of the people in my professional life, and many in my personal life, whom I dearly loved, were never heard from again. But as I mentioned before, over an extended period, new friends, people in the body of Christ embraced me and became integral to the healing process in my life.

Even though I had become paralyzed with fear, my brothers and sisters in Christ stepped in and stepped up. They recognized the attack of the enemy on my life and they surrounded very closely so that while I was injured they tended to the wounds. While I was confused and lost they helped me navigate my way through.

How? My true friends were present with me. They consistently loved me, supported me, and helped me to become more spiritually mature throughout the entire walk through fire. I will share a little information about some of them to demonstrate how we in the body of Christ can minister to others in the fire.

My friends Sue and Elmer had something similar happen to their family years prior when they were falsely accused and were charged criminally in the same state. They were very transparent with me about their personal circumstances. When they saw what was happening to me, they took me under their wings and encouraged me and spent time with me all through the ordeal, even going to court with me on the worst day when I had nobody. Sue would call me like clockwork on the morning each time I went to court and speak strong encouraging words and was there to hold my hand in court on that cold January day when things did not turn out as hoped. Elmer counseled me on how the legal system worked and assured me eventually after ravaging what they could from me they would forget about me and move on to somebody else. We formed a close family bond, and regardless of the sadness at times, we enjoyed our time together and still do. And one thing we discovered is in sharing our journeys together, all of our souls have healed.

My friend Tanya monitored the legal process and was very active helping me find the best legal advice when the initial attorney's with the school had provided ill counsel, taken all my money and withdrew on the eve of trial. Being a former police officer, she fully understood the tactics of each player in the justice system. She educated me on the corruption I was encountering and advised me as best she could. Mostly she was there for me and one of the few old friends that stayed present with me. In fact she was the one that uncovered the misrepresentation I was getting from the original legal counsel and discovered the intent to mislead me in taking a plea deal.

While I was incarcerated, a few friends took care of all the responsibilities regarding my home, finances, and pets. They visited me every week faithfully, affording me a break from the 24/7 chaos and giving me something that I could count on.

My friend Tara, also my pastor's wife, would visit every Thursday no matter what, even though we were only given 15 minutes to visit through opaque scratched up Plexiglas and speak through a phone attached on both sides. She was outraged at the injustice not just because she was my friend, but also because she runs her own school and understands the sacrifices and challenges that accompany people in leadership. Anyone would think this level of sacrifice was too much to request of anyone.

Then there is my best friend Pam. I could see her heart from the first minute we met. It was so refreshing to have a genuine godly and loving person with the capacity for true dedicated friendship to do whatever it takes to really *go through* and *pray through*. I like to tease by telling her that I had to go to jail to get her formally ordained. She has been ministering for years, but it was during this time that Pam finally got her clergy license so that she could come and visit me at the jail as often as possible. Because she was ordained, she was not restricted to the 15-minute time slot. She came on the nonvisiting days, especially when I was going through the hardest times. Two of my other friends were also ordained ministers, so Pam would schedule them and a small group of other friends so that I had regular visitors. And on Sundays my brother always visited. Regardless, Pam came every single week, sometimes more than once a week, and we spoke on the phone every day that inmates had phone privileges.

When I finally got released, I remained in a state of paralysis over a period of many months. At times I was so low I had morbid thoughts bordering on being suicidal. If it had not been for the love of God coming through my friends and family, I do not know if I would have survived. I wanted to leave this world so badly. But over this prolonged walk through fire, because of my friends in the body of Christ, all obstacles were removed, the roof was torn off, and I was placed at the feet of Jesus where I was able to rise, pick up my mat, and go home.

Home for us is simply *the will of God*. While we may go through periods of paralysis from time to time, even if we cannot contain ourselves, we can still choose to remain in the will of God. We can complete the duty of the moment even if a war is erupting in our souls, for His yoke is easy and burden is light (Matthew 11:30), and we can rely upon those friends that God will send us in our moment of need.

*****

In *Walking with God through Pain and Suffering*, Timothy Keller illustrates the suffering of betrayal by analyzing the lives of Paul and Jeremiah. Keller explains that in the Bible, most of Paul's suffering was caused because of his bravery to further the Gospel, similar to the suffering of Jeremiah the prophet. Paul was constantly being beaten, imprisoned, or attacked by his own people as well as by Gentiles. At one place in his letters, Paul gives us a nonexhaustive list in 2 Corinthians 11:23-29 (AMP) of what he had gone through as a messenger of God:

[23] Are they [self-proclaimed] servants of Christ?—I am speaking as if I were out of my mind—I am more so [for I exceed them]; with far more labors, with far more imprisonments, beaten times without number, and often in danger of death. [24] Five times I received from the Jews [a]thirty-nine *lashes*. [25] Three times I was beaten with rods, once I was stoned. Three times I was shipwrecked, a night and a day I have spent *adrift* on the sea; [26] many times on journeys, [exposed to] danger from rivers, danger from bandits, danger from my own countrymen, danger from the Gentiles, danger in the city, danger in the wilderness, danger on the sea, danger among those posing as believers; [27] in labor and hardship, often unable to sleep, in hunger and thirst, often [driven to] fasting [for lack of

food], in cold and exposure [without adequate clothing]. ²⁸ Besides those external things, there is the daily [inescapable] pressure of my concern for all the churches. ²⁹ Who is weak, and I do not feel [his] weakness? Who is made to sin, and I am not on fire [with sorrow and concern]?

Notice what Paul says in the last verse, "...I am not on fire." Paul had been beaten nearly to death and was exposed to danger of every kind, yet he says he was not on fire. He was not heavily burdened with sorrow or concern. How can that be?

Jeremiah also was put in stocks and imprisoned for simply speaking truth to power (Jeremiah 20:1-6). Keller states, "In many parts of the world today, public criticism of the government or of the dominant religious or cultural institutions can get you beaten, imprisoned, or killed. In our culture, it is very possible to become the object of a political attack within your company or neighborhood if you are open about commitment to an unpopular cause.

But it is even more likely that this kind of betrayal happens simply through a personal relationship going sour. When someone perceives that they have been wronged by you, they may embark on a program of trying to hurt you or damage your reputation. Often someone you thought you knew well can turn on you and attack you because it furthers their career or interests. Personal betrayals are particularly horrific and this sort of trial can tempt you to give in to debilitating anger and bitterness."

This kind of suffering will cause us to wrestle with the issues of forgiveness which can become such a stronghold that we become utterly paralyzed. The temptation for us can be to become bitter and to hide the growing hardness and cruelty under the self-image of being a noble victim. Keller states, "Often confrontation and the pursuit of justice is indeed required, but it must be carried out without the spirit of vengefulness." Experiences like this may cause a person to become a worse person rather than a better one.

*****

For us to be able to receive the best of God in our lives going forward, we have work that needs to take place. Forgiveness. That is something that friends cannot help us with although they may try. The good news is that we always have our helper, the Holy Spirit, and we just need to ask.

Corrie Ten Boom, who wrote *The Hiding Place,* recalls forgiving a guard at the concentration camp where her sister died. When she was in a church in Munich she was sharing a message about the forgiveness of God. There, the same guard who had beaten and killed her sister in the concentration camp approached her with his hand thrust out to shake hers and to compliment her message. He acknowledged being a guard in the same camp she was in and told her he had become a Christian. He knew God had forgiven him of the cruel things he did there, but then he asked "Fraulein, will you forgive me?"

As Corrie Ten Boom thought about the man standing before her, she could not forgive. Her sister Betsie had died in that camp and this man could not erase the slow terrible death by simply asking for forgiveness. What seemed like hours, but what was actually seconds later she recalled that as God forgives us we are told to forgive those who have injured us. She thought about the people she knew in Holland who were victims of Nazi brutality. Those who were able to forgive their former enemies were able also to return to the outside world and rebuild their lives, no matter the physical scars. Those who nursed their bitterness remained invalids. It was as simple and horrible as that. She recounts, "And still I stood there with the coldness clutching my heart, but forgiveness is not an emotion – I knew that too. Forgiveness is an act of the will, and the will can function regardless of the temperature of the heart." At that moment she silently prayed, "Jesus, help me!" Then she decided she could at least lift her hand to shake the hand of the former guard. Still, she knew God would have to supply the feeling. As she thrust her hand toward the man, a current flowed through her and a healing warmth came over her entire being, bringing tears to her eyes. And she said, "I forgive you brother with all my heart!"

Having the experience of forgiving the Nazi guard did not cause Corrie Ten Boom to master all issues of forgiveness. Throughout life, she found herself struggling with betrayal of Christian friends, and was not able to stop hurtful reverberating thoughts of how she was hurt. So she again had to ask for help. In this experience she learned that we can trust God not only above our emotions, but also above our thoughts.

Corrie Ten Boom struggled with forgiveness even though she had overcome more than most of us can imagine because it was the people she loved who injured her in this situation. We can all relate to this.

What troubled me most was not the evil tapestry of enemies, but the silence of friends. The deeper wounds did not come from those who were known adversaries, but they came from those I loved who hurt me in secret.

On the day I was released and we drove across the bridge away from Ohio, a place I once loved that I had come to detest, I remember having one particular realization. I knew if I did not leave any bitterness, hatred, or unforgiveness behind, I would remain in a state of paralysis.

Let us again declare our Overcomer's Creed:

> I will get through this because God is with me.
>
> My walk through fire may be painful,
>
> And it may be long,
>
> But with God's help I will overcome.
>
> In the meantime, I will be wise and hopeful because
>
> God will use IT for good.

TEN

Intellectual Faith

Atrocities like the Holocaust; violence in Cambodia, Rwanda, Sudan, and other countries; or our own personal atrocities have the handwriting of the one who comes to steal, kill, and destroy; but we can find the signature of God when we experience peace, love, joy and abundant life. Yes, in these things we find the handwriting of God.

– Dr. Lisa

The intensity of walking through fire can cause us to question what we believe and why we believe it. This chapter ministers specifically to people who need someone to walk with them through the confusion and doubt we sometimes experience in the fire. It is especially written for those who have been through horrific traumas too difficult to process. If this describes any of us, you are not alone. Know that faith and intellect are both necessary in this world in your walk with God.

For most of us, at some point in our lives, we will go through fire. Whether we say it out loud or not, we will think to ourselves, *where is God?*

Job 30:26 says, ²⁶*Yet when I hoped for good, evil came; when I looked for light, then came darkness* (NIV). Job looked everywhere but could not see God.

In the walk through fire we often cannot see Him so we begin to question. Where is He in this situation? Where is He in this crisis? Where is He in this relationship? Where is He in these financial problems? Where is He in our problems with our children? Where is He with this illness?

When we begin to ask these types of questions, there is evidence that our faith has been put on trial.

I read the book of Job over and over again during the most difficult parts of my walk through fire. This last time I approached Job with an open mind, hoping to see something that I had never seen before, something that would lead me to a new understanding.

Sages are people who have attained wisdom in understanding how others think. They tell us that Job instructs, "God is like a mirror. The mirror never changes, but everyone who looks at it sees a different face." This means that when individuals read the book of Job, they find it confirms what they already want to believe. They see themselves in the book and interpret it in whatever way seems to benefit them best.

The book of Job presents the issue of good people suffering in a world under God's control. Job is the innocent who has become the victim. In Job's walk through fire, he encountered friends who made the mental anguish Job was experiencing much worse. It is possible we will have experiences with people just like the friends of Job. These types of people may think they know more than they really do and often make ridiculous claims all in the name of religion. Some of the most familiar ones are *none of us are perfect, we are all sinners, so God will punish all of us eventually, some sooner than later.* In other words, *he must have done something to deserve it.*

Before even considering these kinds of responses, we need to think about how we would respond to the parents of a child who has died. Is there anything that *anybody* could do to deserve the death of a child? What answer would we accept? Even though it may be well intended, it is really rubbing salt in the wounds when people makes statements like "he's in a better place now," "at least you had him for X years," or "someday you will understand why this was the right thing to happen." We should avoid any of these responses.

What answer would we give to the survivors of the Holocaust? I imagine some of the responses they have been given infuriate them. There are some religious people who feel the need to justify the atrocity at the expense of the martyrs of Auschwitz and the Warsaw Ghetto, saying things like "it was God's punishment of the Jews for forsaking the traditional ways." Those same people who say this do not realize that many of the victims were Jews who had not forsaken traditional ways. Even if they had forsaken traditional ways, is a firing squad or a gas chamber appropriate punishment for working on the Sabbath? Or they may say, "It was God's way of shaming the nations of the world and establishing the state of Israel," as if an omnipotent God could not find a less bloodthirsty way of bringing that about.

*****

It has been more than 70 years since the end of World War II, but it is hard to estimate the impact of the Holocaust on people's ability to have faith in God and in God's Word. Countless people completely lost their faith and said they no longer believed in God. Some because they resented the idea of an authority telling them what they could or could not do. But in the overwhelming majority of cases, people lost faith in God because of the many loved ones lost at war or other untimely death of someone they love; because of Hitler; because of atrocities in Cambodia, Rwanda, Sudan, and other countries; because of pain and suffering; or because they look at the evil in the world, and they cannot believe in the existence of an all-powerful, loving, caring, and giving God in charge of things.

Rabbi Shapira was a much beloved rabbi of the Warsaw Ghetto, and he was a leader of a small Hasidic community near Warsaw before the Second World War. In Rabbi Harold Kushner's book, *The Book of Job: When Bad Things Happened to a Good Person*, he shares a sermon delivered by Rabbi Shapira in November 1939 shortly after the Nazis invaded Poland and began murdering Jews. The rabbi connected this atrocity to the familiar story found in Genesis 22 in which Abraham, as we will remember, is commanded to offer his son Isaac as a sacrifice, only to have the boy spared at the last moment. One can understand why that story would be on the minds of Polish Jews in November 1939. But Rabbi Shapira did not invoke the story to tell his congregation to have faith in God who would intervene at the last moment to spare them. Instead, the rabbi connected the story to the first verse of chapter 23, which tells of the death of Abraham's wife, Sarah. He cited a well-known rabbinic tradition that Sarah died of shock and grief when she realized how close her son had come to dying. The rabbi then went on to address a sermon directly to God. In an act of astonishing boldness, he told God that Sarah's faith would ordinarily have been strong enough to survive that ordeal, but that she willed herself to die to warn God of the consequences of letting such things happen. If God did not stop the Nazis, many people's faith would not be up to the test, and they would abandon God and Judaism.

God can do whatever He wants to do, but God does not hurt his children. What God does is out of love and that is where we find evidence of His movement. Atrocities like the Holocaust; violence in Cambodia, Rwanda, Sudan, and other countries; or our own personal atrocities have the handwriting of the one who comes to steal, kill, and destroy, but we can find the signature of God when we experience peace, love, joy, and abundant life. Yes, in these things we find the handwriting of God.

*****

Bad things do happen to good people, but there definitely is an all-powerful, loving, caring, and giving God in charge of all things. How do we reconcile the questions we have when we have experienced such atrocities? At some point we all go on a quest for answers to very difficult questions. We may not have all the answers but the cross of Christ does give us some answers. We can eliminate the question of His love for us, and the question of why He does not end the suffering for us. The cross of Christ overwhelmingly demonstrates the depth of God's love for us, and that He also has suffered so that we might live. In seasons of our lives when questions arise, we must remember to turn to God and not away from God, seeking the answers from the all-knowing One with the nail scarred hands.

*****

Rabbi Harold Kushner spent many years counseling people and guiding them to answers to questions raised at times of trial and tribulation. But when faced with his own walk through fire, he had his own sets of questions. His son Aaron was diagnosed with progeria, a rapid aging disease, on the same day his daughter was born. On that day, which was truly one of the best and the worst in his life, the rabbi found out that his son would not grow taller than 3 feet, would have no hair on his head, would look like a tiny old man when he was still a child, and would die in his early teens. With a deep aching sense of unfairness, Rabbi Kushner decided to explore those difficult questions and in the process he wrote *Why Do Bad Things Happen to Good People?* His conclusion is that everyone has been hurt by life (not God) – by death, illness, injury, rejection or disappointment – and even if we cannot make sense of the pain and suffering of life, the key is to turn to God for strength and comfort. And among the many profound expressions, Rabbi Kushner argues when suffering, our question should not be, "God, why are You doing this to me?" but rather "God, see what is happening to me. Can You help me?"

*****

Often, the beloved stories of the Bible we have known for years can be perceived in a much different manner when we are forced to contend with the atrocities of life. But I believe God has put them there in preparation for times when we walk through fire.

What exactly do we believe is God's role in the pain and suffering of life?

Many spectacular images of God exist such as that of a creator, healer, provider, protector, deliverer, and much more revealed in His many names and attributes. Yet, why do we begin to see negative attributes when walking through fire? Why do we begin to imagine faulty views contradictory to what the Word of God tells us about the character of God?

The false image of God the punisher is usually provoked by those with a religious or judgmental spirit, usually in the name of religion. These people offer negative judgments despite Christ's admonition not to judge and empty clichés like the aforementioned ones to parents whose child has died. Those are thoughts we should never think and statements we should never speak.

God's hiding face is a false image we may have when we feel God allows harm to come to us. We may believe terrible things happen to people, not because God wills them, but because God is upset with the people and turns His attention from them, leaving them unprotected against the power of evil. God loves His people and even though from time to time He may be dismayed by their misbehavior, He promises that He will never forsake us.

A busy and forgetful God is another fallacy. The thought that God is too busy with more important problems in the world to pay attention to our misfortunes does not come from God. He has not directed his attention away from us. Some have wrongly stated that God has not seen the cruelty that has taken place in humanity so He has failed to protect us.

God is not the superhero with specialized powers in one area and limitations in another. He is all powerful and all knowing.

God is not the evil genius sitting behind a big screen creating catastrophes throughout the universe when He sees something that disappoints Him.

And God is certainly not the retired hero of a Western movie who can be prevailed upon to come to the rescue of an innocent by a combination of desperate pleas and flattery.

Any characteristic described about God that is not in the Word of God is not true. Bottom line.

A surprising number of biblical scholars come to the end of Job and decide that the author's answer is that there is none. God's ways remain a mystery, beyond our understanding. God and the ways of His kingdom are mysterious. At times God does make known His mysteries in ways that we can understand, but it is only through an intimate relationship that He will reveal Himself.

For the times His ways remain a mystery, we must heed the wisdom of Solomon in Proverbs 3:5-6 which says, "Trust in the Lord with all your heart and lean not on your own understanding; in all your ways acknowledge him and he shall direct your paths" (NKJV).

The Scriptures tell us, "15 But in your hearts set Christ apart [as holy—acknowledging Him, giving Him first place in your lives] as Lord. Always be ready to give a [logical] defense to anyone who asks you to account for the hope *and* confident assurance [elicited by faith] that is within you, yet [do it] with gentleness and respect" (1 Peter 3:15 AMP.)

*****

The study of Apologetics is using evidence to build a defense for something. In this case we need to build evidence for our belief in God and the basis for our faith and God's Word. When we do we will come to know belief in God is reasonable and well evidenced. It is not based on feelings. Jesus is a real person, who is really God, and who has the solution to humanity's problems. Oftentimes in the fire we can lose confidence in what we believe.

But when we do, we must dig deeply into the Word to find the answers that God has documented for us. God has chosen each scripture to be written in the Bible so that we would have what we need to have the abundant life He came to give us.

In the teaching series *Why Do You Believe That?* Apologist Mary Jo Sharp states, "Belief in the goodness of God is not a whim or a feeling, but it is the actual truth in our lives. We as Christians need to discover the real answers to our honest questions. We need to become sufficiently adept at handling the truth so we can feel confident, and we need to be about the job of sharing the truth, especially with those in pain walking through fire. We must tell everyone the reason for our hope. We must be able to give an answer to doubts with solid intellectual ground to stand on."

When we go through trials, we must understand that it is normal to question our faith. Even committed Christians question their faith and wonder at times if what they have believed is true.

In Luke 7, John the Baptist questioned his faith in Jesus. John had seen the miraculous appearance of the Holy Spirit at the baptism of Jesus, yet in prison John doubted so much he sent men to ask if Jesus was really the Messiah (see verse 20).

Jesus didn't rebuke John for asking this question. He didn't say, "John, you just need to have more faith." Instead, Jesus provided evidence of His identity. He made a case (a defense) to establish His identity by healing people.

We can make a case for belief in God to answer the doubts of believers. To have doubts is alright, but we need to take sufficient steps toward alleviating them. Christians who have grown up in the church may not have even begun to answer the questions that plague them. Yet, many go from a childhood acceptance of the Christian faith (based on the confidence and trust in leaders such as their parents, pastors, etc.) to a mature faith based on their own belief and intimacy with God.

Does answering doubts and offering reasons for belief in God take away faith in God?

Is stronger faith the answer to doubt?

Answering doubts or questions can build confidence. After I began to answer some of my most pressing questions, I discovered that the Bible had the best answers to my toughest questions. When I began comparing, I found that Christianity made the most sense as a worldview. As I began to investigate my beliefs more deeply while walking through fire, I built more confidence in what it was I believe and knew I could change more lives as a result. I knew the process had changed me and I knew it would change others given the opportunity.

The term faith *has* become somewhat convoluted in our current culture. It seems to mean that believing something is true despite the evidence or lack of evidence. However, a faith not based on knowledge of God, including physical as well as supernatural evidence, is not the faith described in the Bible.

Hebrews 11:6 states,

"⁶But without faith *it is* impossible to please Him, for he who comes to God must believe that He is, and *that* He is a rewarder of those who diligently seek Him" (NKJV).

A person of faith has to first believe in the existence of God. How many people have an anemic faith because they have not feasted on the evidence? The passage of Scripture continues to determine God's physical interactions with his creation.

Theologian J. Gresham Machen said it this way:

Faith is indeed intellectual; it involves an apprehension of certain things as facts; and vain is the modern effort to divorce faith from knowledge, but although faith is intellectual, it is not *only* intellectual. You cannot have faith *without* having knowledge; but you will not have faith if you have *only* knowledge.

Scholars at the Creation Museum in Petersburg, Kentucky have said, "Broadly speaking, man's word refers to autonomous reasoning – the idea that the human mind can determine truth independently from

God's revealed truth, the Bible. Reasoning is God's gift to humankind, but He has instructed us to use the Bible as our ultimate starting point (Proverbs 1:7) and also to reject speculations that contradict God's knowledge (2 Corinthians 10:5). Philosophies and world religions that use human guesses rather than God's Word as a starting point are prone to misinterpret the facts around them because their starting point is arbitrary. Every person must make a choice. Individuals must choose God's Word as the starting point for all their reasoning, or start their own arbitrary philosophy for evaluating everything around them including how they view the Bible."

As we saw in Hebrews 11:6, to draw near to God, we must believe that He exists. To experience the fruit of faith, we have to get back to something as fundamental as believing in God's existence because "people may not always live what they profess, but they will always live what they believe."

There may come a time in our lives that doubt raises in our minds and we might believe God is some grand hoax. When that happens, studying what we believe and why we believe it in advance gives us ammunition to know that we have a whole body of evidence to the contrary. We will have the ammunition when called upon to make a public case for belief that there is a good God who loves us and who is working on our behalf to give us a full and abundant life.

Now God will give us individual revelations when we have intimate walks with Him, but He will not show us anything contradictory to the current scripture.

The Apostle Paul told the early Christians that there were some revelations he received that he could not tell us because they were too weighty. He said we would not be able to understand them. We can only understand what he did write by the spirit but certainly not of his own intellect. So what did he not write?

This is the same apostle that was called up to the third heaven. This guy knew theology. The Holy Spirit used him to pen most of the theology of the New Testament and this is what he says in 1 Corinthians 3:1-3:

"However, brothers and sisters, I could not talk to you as to spiritual people, but [only] as to [a]worldly people [dominated by human nature], *mere* infants [in the new life] in Christ! ² I fed you with milk, not solid food; for you were not yet able *to receive it.* Even now you are still not ready. ³ You are still [b]worldly [controlled by ordinary impulses, the sinful capacity]. For as long as there is jealousy and strife *and* discord among you, are you not [c]unspiritual, and are you not walking like ordinary men [unchanged by faith]?" (AMP)

The guidelines we need to understand the Word of God are given in 2 Timothy 2:15:

¹⁵"Be diligent to present yourself approved to God, a worker who does not need to be ashamed, rightly dividing the word of truth" (NKJV).

Rightly dividing, or hermeneutics, means to:

- Read scripture in context.
- Know who is speaking.
- Know to whom the scripture is speaking – the Jews, the nations, or the church.
- Remember that Scripture will agree with other Scriptures.

Hebrews 5:11-6:1 warns us about becoming dull learners.

¹¹ About this we have much to say, and it is hard to explain, since you have become dull of hearing. ¹² For though by this time you ought to be teachers, you need someone to teach you again the basic principles of the oracles of God. You need milk, not solid food, ¹³ for everyone who lives

on milk is unskilled in the word of righteousness, since he is a child. ¹⁴ But solid food is for the mature, for those who have their powers of discernment trained by constant practice to distinguish good from evil. ⁶ Therefore let us leave the elementary doctrine of Christ and go on to maturity, not laying again a foundation of repentance from dead works and of faith toward God (ESV).

We have to be committed to seek God. Bible scholars are those aspiring to higher learning in the things of God.

Dull learners are people not wanting to learn difficult things. John 16:33 (AMP) says,

³³ I have told you these things, so that in Me you may have [perfect] peace. In the world you have tribulation and distress and suffering, but be courageous [be confident, be undaunted, be filled

with joy]; I have overcome the world." [My conquest is accomplished, My victory abiding.]

Here we can see that Jesus warns us that we will have trouble but He also tells us that we have no worries because He has overcome the world.

Suffering is the result of human sin. The world is not the way that God created it. Because of that, all are vulnerable to the effects of sin in the world.

Why does one person suffer and another does not? Why do catastrophes happen to some and not to others?

It is because sin is in the world.

But there will come a day when the Lord will return and cleanse this world of all sin and all suffering as Revelation 21:4 says:

"And God shall wipe away all tears from their eyes; and there shall be no more death, neither sorrow, nor crying, neither shall there be any more pain: for the former things are passed away" (KJV).

Together again:

I will get through this because God is with me.

My walk through fire may be painful,

And it may be long,

But with God's help I will overcome.

In the meantime, I will be wise and hopeful because

God will use *IT* for good.

*For more on Apologetics and dispelling fallacies see the *Walking Through Fire* Bible Study Series.

ELEVEN

Wise Humility

Wise and humble people acknowledge those limitations and do not allow their happiness to be destroyed. Some things just have to be left to God. After all, God reserves His right as the Universal Doctor of Jurisprudence and He will vindicate those who have been treated unjustly.

—Dr. Lisa

Bridge building in its early days was very dangerous, and construction workers were well aware of that fact. Up high in the air, the workers were buffeted by the wind, which made their scaffolds sway. Newspapers called such conditions the "dance of danger." Engineers even calculated the fatality rate. They had estimated that there would be one life lost for every $1 million spent. If $40 million spent, 40 people were likely to die, which is just the way it was. In 1932 the builders of the Golden Gate Bridge thought they could do better to save lives and put in some safety measures. Although the biggest measure that saved the most lives was very new to bridge building, it was very old to the circus. A trapeze net! It cost $130,000 and was 60 feet below the roadbed of the bridge. The safety net went out on all the sides and it was so successful that the newspapers kept a running box score. Gate bridge safety net: 8 – lives lost: 0.

A running tally was kept. Nineteen men fell into the net and their lives were saved. The survivors were known as members of the Halfway to Hell Club. Some of us are also on the Halfway to Hell Club. We have all been in this club at some point. Yet the most amazing thing about the laborers saved by the safety net was that all the workers said that they were free from the paralyzing fear of falling to their death and became more effective and joyful in their work. This story reminds me of God's grace net – Jesus Christ. When we finally get so worn out we cannot hold on any longer, we let go and God catches us. He holds us in His arms. Not only does He catch us in His grace net, but He also begins the healing and restoration process in our lives. We look to Isaiah 53-5: "But He was pierced for our rebellion, crushed for our sins. He was beaten so we could be whole. He was whipped so we could be healed" (NLT).

Let us focus on the words *whole* and *healed* in this passage. The prophet Isaiah foretold of the Messiah coming to the cross and taking on our brokenness. When Christ's side was pierced by the sword, the Scripture says blood and water flowed from His side. Some medical experts believe that was a sign that His heart had burst. So Jesus Christ died literally from a broken heart so that our hearts could be restored. He was broken so that we can find restoration. James 4:6 says, "God resists the proud, but gives grace to the humble" (NKJV).

Grace, if we but knew it, is really the power to change. That grace net frees us from paralyzing fear and puts us in an atmosphere we can change with God's power. But not only does God catch us in the grace net when we let go of the bridge of control, He begins that healing process as we let Him heal us and fill us every day. However, the first step we have to admit is that we are powerless. The Bible says He gives grace to the humble. Humble are those who admit they need that grace, those who admit that they need His power to change, and this is a daily process.

*****

Solomon became king at age 12. The Lord appeared to him in a dream and told him to ask for whatever he wanted and He would give it to him.

So what do we notice here?

First the Lord Himself appeared to Solomon rather than an angel on assignment.

Second, the Lord God asked Solomon to make a request. God did not say, "Hey, you are a kid and you don't know what you are doing, so this is what I'm going to give you because you need it." No, Solomon was told by God to ask. Food for thought...

Interestingly enough, Solomon asked for Wisdom. A kid asking for wisdom – certainly a God thing.

So God granted Solomon's request for wisdom in every sense of the word.

We find that Solomon's intellectual powers far surpassed anything known in his time, described as wisdom, great understanding, and broadness of mind. Not only did Solomon possess the wisdom to make appropriate judgments in matters of dispute, but he was also broadly educated and extremely insightful in observation and analysis. In a word, he was smart.

Both Egypt and Mesopotamia already had impressive reputations in wisdom and intellectual matters. Significant writing and collecting of proverbs had already been done in both areas. Books similar to Job, Ecclesiastes, and Song of Solomon had been published by wisdom writers of Egypt and Mesopotamia. It is likely that Solomon received instruction in such matters from the Egyptian consultants that he had brought in to help shape his government. If so, he proved an apt pupil, outstripping his teachers. It was declared that he had outdone Egypt and the East. Yet, Solomon, just like the rest of us spent his time in the fire. How did *IT* affect him?

For a moment, let us track King Solomon's own search for happiness in life. One of the things Solomon learned is that life gives us circumstances that make us humble.

How do we face life with humility?

Solomon taught that life has its own way of humbling us. When life touches every area of our living, sooner or later it will, and by some measure, bring us to our knees.

Abraham Lincoln said, "I have been driven many times upon my knees by the overwhelming conviction that I had nowhere else to go. My own wisdom and that of all about me seemed insufficient for that day."

God says above all things that we need to learn how to walk humbly with Him. God not only says that He wants us to be in relationship with Him and to walk with Him, but He describes what He wants the walk to look like.

Even though Solomon certainly questioned God and had many fire walks, he operated with humility towards God out of wisdom. Humility has been described as a Christian grace or virtue. It is defined as freedom from pride and arrogance; a modest estimation of our own worth.

*****

We often think of humility as softness or weakness or compliance, yet those words do not describe Christ nor do they describe the kind of person King Solomon talks about in Proverbs and Ecclesiastes.

In his book *Searching for Heaven on Earth*, Dr. David Jeremiah did a study on the eighth chapter of Ecclesiastes which defines humility in five ways:

1. Knowing how much we do not know
2. Living with what we do not like
3. Accepting what we cannot change
4. Enjoying what we cannot explain
5. Discovering what we cannot discover

We have seen throughout history many who refuse to adopt humility as a personal virtue. According to Svetlana Stalin, her father, Josef Stalin, while on his death bed clenched his fist toward heaven, and fell back on his pillow dead. Sometimes when we look throughout the world historically we have seen people shaking their fists in the face of God. And they are saying, "I've lived like this my whole life, and nothing has happened to me yet and nothing's going to happen to me. I am the captain of my soul and the master of my life."

Nelson Mandela repeated the famous line: "I am the captain of my soul!" Mandela suffered 27 years in prison before becoming South Africa's president and leading his nation peacefully from apartheid to democracy.

While imprisoned, he contracted tuberculosis, survived long bouts of solitary confinement, and was kept from attending his son's funeral. For several years, he was only permitted one visit and letter every six months.

How did Nelson Mandela not only survive but thrive?

How is it that he was able to smile so infectiously for the entire world to see?

How is it that he became one of the most effective world changers and history makers?

During the long years of Mandela's confinement, he came to cherish William Ernest Henley's poem, "Invictus." It's title was given to a 2009 movie with Morgan Freeman in the role of Mandela.

In the Denison Forum on Truth and Culture, Jim Denison wrote, *Nelson Mandela: I am the Captain of my Soul* highlighting the significance of this poem to

Mandela and explained how He often recited it to fellow inmates.

Here's the text of Mandela's favorite poem:

Out of the night that covers me,
Black as the pit from pole to pole,
I thank whatever gods may be
For my unconquerable soul.
In the fell clutch of circumstance
I have not winced nor cried aloud.
Under the bludgeonings of chance
My head is bloody, but unbowed.
Beyond this place of wrath and tears
Looms but the Horror of the shade,
And yet the menace of the years
Finds and shall find me unafraid.
It matters not how strait the gate,
How charged with punishments the scroll,
I am the master of my fate,
I am the captain of my soul.

Denison stated, the famous poem had a remarkable author, William Ernest Henley. Henley wrote about his "unconquerable" soul likely because at the age of 12, he contracted tuberculosis of the bone, a disease that led to the amputation of his left leg, below the knee, when he was around 20 years old. Over time his right foot became diseased as well, leading to a three-year stay in the hospital. He died of tuberculosis at age 53.

The poem obviously inspired Nelson Mandela and helped strengthen him during horrifying suffering. But we do have to be very cautious not to take every element of this poem literally. Some of the thoughts actually misguide the reader.

There are not "gods" that "may be," but one God who is. Our soul is not "unconquerable"—to the contrary, when the King of Kings and Lord of Lords returns to the planet he created (Revelation 19:16), "every knee will bow, in heaven, on earth, and below. And every tongue will confess 'Jesus, the Anointed One, is Lord,' to the glory of God our Father!" (Philippians 2:10-11). I am not "the master of my fate" or "the captain of my soul." Rather, "we must all appear before the judgment seat of Christ, so that each one may receive what is due for what he has done in the body, whether good or evil" (2 Corinthians 5:10, ESV).

On that fateful day, what will matter is not what I think of myself, but what my Master thinks of me. *Invictus* inspired Nelson Mandela to reject his tyrannical government's claim to be the "captain" of his soul. However, his well-documented and sincere commitment to Christ taught him the larger truth: we must keep our soul "unconquered" by all but Jesus. As Dr. Jeremiah has stated, "We do live in a generation that wants to go its own way, thinking we know better than the ancient wisdom of God and His people. We think money, popularity, pleasure, and as with Solomon "vanities" have suddenly become wise choices."

You know we have grown used to living in a culture where people would try to sell us a solution for every problem, but there will always be things we cannot know, things we do not like, things we cannot change, things we cannot explain and things we cannot discover the answer to. That is just life. Wise and humble people acknowledge those limitations and do not allow their happiness to be destroyed. Some things just have to be left to God. After all, God reserves His right as the Universal Doctor of Jurisprudence and He will vindicate those who have been treated unjustly. This suggests having a relationship with Him. And our role as members of the body of Christ is to encourage others who do not know God to consider knowing God through His son Jesus Christ and to help those who do know God grow in the grace and knowledge of Him for a deeper, richer walk as described in Micah 6:8:

> He has shown you, O mortal, what is good.
> And what does the LORD require of you?
> To act justly and to love mercy
> and to **walk humbly** with your God. (NIV)

It is not difficult to walk humbly when we truly understand the greatness of God and the purest example of humility when He came in the form of a man to suffer and die so that we might have life. Surely we can commit to walk humbly before Him and before man.

Ready.

> I will get through this because God is with me.
>
> My walk through fire may be painful,
>
> And it may be long,
>
> But with God's help I will overcome.
>
> In the meantime, I will be wise and hopeful because
>
> God will use IT for good.

*For more study on the Wisdom of Solomon see the *Walking Through Fire* Bible Study Series.

TWELVE

Spirit-Led Approach

The spirit can discern what the mind cannot understand.

– Dr. Lisa

A world renowned Christian communicator and pastor was diagnosed with throat cancer last year. After he was given this devastating news, he had to undergo radiation treatments every day for 28 days. In that time, he was hearing voices from the enemy telling him he would neither speak nor preach again. The enemy told him everything he did in life up until now would be over and "his ministries would collapse and [he would] never again take a microphone in one hand and a Bible in another. Though the message was so terrible, I have always said if the Gospel does not work (in crisis) then it does not work at all," Rod Parsley testified. The spirit-led person who questioned why bad things happen to good people found a completely different answer. In the middle of this crisis, Rod Parsley modeled how the spirit-led individual approaches a crisis, a walk through fire.

First, what does it mean to be led by the spirit?

Basically it is walking under the leadership of God, understanding that He is our divine Guide. Romans 8:14 states those being led by the Spirit of God are the sons of God.

Some people rely strictly on their intellectual abilities to question God, and when they do they come up short. Those who may be intellectuals but rely on the leading of the Holy Spirit instead of their own thoughts when they question, will likely get much different answers.

Why is there a difference? The Spirit can discern what the mind cannot understand.

How does the spirit-led person think about the question, "Why do bad things happen to good people?" Minister Brian Carn gave the explanation that it was because the first man Adam messed up and brought sin to the earth so we are now operating on Satan's lease.

Humankind was created to be the beneficiary to enjoy all of God's goodness but man sinned against God and because of that we are in a fallen world. This is not the way God wants it to be. Why is it fallen? Why does it seem God is doing nothing about it (until Kingdom come?)

God gave this earth to humankind but He did not make us robots. Joseph Prince, Senior Pastor of New Creation Church, in Singapore, explains if we were made like robots we would not have a fallen earth because God would be in control of everyone but God did not want that. He wanted us to have free choice. To have free choice entails risk. God made everything good in the garden except for one tree. God said just to show genuine love for Him there must be a choice. If God surrounds man with only everything good there is no free choice. Why did God not stop Adam and Eve from the sin? If He did, there would not have been free choice. That would not have been just or righteous if God did. God never meant for people to die or grow old or to experience any of the awful things life can bring. God says my people are destroyed for lack of knowledge. When we sin we give the devil a legal right. Sin is saying to the devil that we bow to him and believe him we do not believe God.

God sent His Son to take away the legal right of the devil to hold us captive. Jesus paid the price of sin by the shedding of His blood. The cross was the place where the love of God paid a ransom to the justice of God. Galatians 3:13 says, Christ has redeemed us from the curse of the law. Deuteronomy 28 lists all of the blessings from verses 1-13. Then from verse 14-68 it starts with a warning and then lists all the numerous curses. Why are the curses listed in detail? Is it because we know when we have the blessing but we do not know when we have been cursed? We need to identify them and remember that Jesus freed us from all of it. When we are in a pit, Jesus wants to get us out.

In the natural world, in the earth realm right now, God is looking for people who are in place and in tune with Him so we are able to spiritually discern and stop attacks from the enemy before they come.

If I were to ask you right now if gospel music were in the room you were in, you would say no, (unless you happen to be reading while you are playing music.) But if someone brought a radio in the room and tuned the station to a gospel music station frequency, then I would be right wouldn't I? What made the difference? The music was already in the room. You were just not tuned into the right frequency. That is how it is in the spirit realm. We need to be tuned in to the frequency of the Holy Spirit.

*****

When unjust attacks come upon our lives, at times, if we are tuned into the right frequency of the Holy Spirit, we can experience the miraculous from God. After experiencing the loss of a child, Author and Bible Teacher, Perry Stone, has said that God told him not to question why it happened and his revelation seemed to come from questions of eternity and a prophetic and teaching anointing. But in an interview with a fellow minister, Author Walter Hallam, we find there was a much different result as he was led by the spirit while suffering the loss of his child. Hallam lost his daughter in an airplane crash and through the process of his grief and pain he continued to be led by the spirit and had an encounter with Jesus, either through a visitation, or by seeing in the spirit, he was not certain. Hallam testifies, in his encounter, Jesus gave him revelation from Luke Chapter 13 that illustrates reasons people die and why something bad can happen to people who are good. In his book, *The Big Why?*, Hallam shares the four reasons he said Jesus revealed to him as cults and bad governments, the curse, lack of diligence, and evil spirits.

Firstly, Jesus told him bad governments and the occult because these two entities create martyrs.

Secondly, there is a curse in operation in the earth and accidents can happen because of the curse that was released in the Garden of Eden. Hallam stated that Jesus explained that accidents can happen to spirit filled people because we live in a fallen realm. Most of the time faith will overcome but in rare occasions faith will fail, but will have its largest triumph by gaining Heaven because the world is not worthy of certain people of faith as in Hebrews 11.

Thirdly, If men fail to do their job correctly, if they are complacent, lazy, and do not work with excellence, they can open the door for the curse. Diligence helps keep the door closed.

And finally, there are demonic forces that try to attack and there is a warfare that goes on.

In Hallam's case he did receive answers to the many questions he had reeling. What was different in this circumstance? Dig into Luke 13 again. It is quite clear that Hallam received divine revelation on Word that had been available to us since we have had Bibles at our fingertips.

Have you ever received those four answers in this chapter explaining why bad things happen to the people of God?

No. Me either.

Thank God for His divine revelation when He chooses to give it.

There is something to be said about being spirit led.

*****

It is absolutely critical that we are tuned in so that we can stop the attacks from the enemy preemptively.

How can we stop it? Through prayer.

The enemy is the god of this world and we have to take back the dominion God gave us in this world. God can do nothing on earth without human invitation and interaction. There must be someone on earth who is cooperating with God.

Ezekiel said, "I sought for a man that will stand in the gap and make up the hedge." The problem was nobody could be found.

Second Corinthians 2:11 tells us, *¹¹"to keep Satan from taking advantage of us; for we are not ignorant of his schemes." (AMP)* That Scripture shows us something very profound. It shows us that it is possible for us to be saved, sanctified, and filled with the Holy Ghost, on fire and in love with the Lord, and Satan can still have an advantage. He can have the advantage through our ignorance or lack of awareness. When we do not know how he operates, he can take us off guard and use that advantage. When we do not know that someone is planning to do evil, they have an advantage. For example, if someone is planning to burglarize a house and the owners do not know it, the burglars have an advantage. So that is why when we can hear from God it gives us an advantage.

It is critical that we develop a close walk with God so we learn to discern what He is saying. It is also critical that we have close relationships with others who can hear from God. We need the advantage God makes available to us so we are able to see traps and snares before they ever come.

Some Christians with experience in spiritual warfare believe the enemy is not just after us personally, but he is after entire territories and regions. Territorial spirits can be described as demons that are believed to hang over certain geographical areas. That used to be hard for me to believe until I experienced personal effects of territorial spirits.

There is no doubt in my mind now, in hindsight, that there were all kinds of territorial spirits around the schools I started and developed in the inner city. The level of warfare getting the schools going was intense enough, but for a time, a peace seemed to come over the area and the schools greatly prospered. But the last five years I was there, the warfare grew more intense than ever, and I did not discern what was happening until it was too late. I was simply not armed enough for battle to breakdown the strongholds, and I certainly did not have adequate spiritual support systems at the time. Most importantly, I did not have a covering of prayer. I have since learned from that lesson. When going into battle in the enemy's territory, we need to be covered 360 degrees in prayer. We need to have mature saints around us that can get a word to the throne room of God and can discern what is going on at all times in the spirit realm.

*****

Today there is an unprecedented attempt to silence truth, kill joy, murder peace and bury hope. The objective is simple, capture whatever carries God's presence and create a stronghold.

The threats against our faith globally are very serious. We know we stand in the midst of a great spiritual battle. In a message entitled, *When Light Stands Next to Darkness, Light Always Wins*, Pastor Samuel Rodriguez says, "Forget Harry Potter and Hogwarts. Via the conduit of biblical illusions we know very well there are real spirits in the cities of the world today. The spirit of Pharaoh is alive, holding people captive in the Egypt of bondage and fear. The spirit of Goliath still lives mocking and intimidating the children of God. The spirit of Jezebel still makes men and women hide in caves with sexual perversion and manipulation. The spirit of Absalom is still alive dividing homes, churches, and relationships, while the spirit of Herod is killing the young through violence, poverty, and sex trafficking, murdering infant dreams and visions."

There is a spiritual battle out there. Yet, there is great news. There is a spirit more powerful than all of these spirits combined. The most powerful spirit alive on the planet today is still the Holy Spirit of God.

Rodriguez challenges the spirit led person to "rise up with spiritual fortitude and prophetic courage. We need to rise up and declare with a smile on our faces and joy in our step, to every narrative and spirit that facilitates a platform of moral relativism, of spiritual apathy, of cultural decadence, and ecclesiastical lukewarmness, we must declare, regardless of what is happening, we must declare that for every Pharaoh there will be a Moses. For every Goliath there must be a David. For every Nebuchadnezzar there must be a Daniel. For every Jezebel there must be an Elijah. For every Herod there must be a Jesus. And for every devil that rises up against you, there is a mightier God that will rise up for you! That is the gospel of Jesus and that my friend is the power of God!"

Many of us have been under assault because the enemy wants to capture all things glorious. We can literally feel dissipation of our joy, peace, and integrity. Why? Because the enemy is threatened by the future God has planned for us. This is not about what we have done in the past but about what we are about to do and the enemy is attempting to stop it.

This is why we must be spirit led. This time we are not going through this fire to escape. We are going through this fire to get to the greatest season of our lives.

Proverbs 23:18 says, "For without a doubt, there is a future and it will not be cut off." (BBE)

To get to the greatest season of our lives and to walk in victory, we have to understand and identify strongholds. Can we believe the enemy has strongholds over us that need to be broken? A description of a stronghold is something that has a "strong hold" over a person. A person seems to have no control over it and cannot seem to stop doing it. It can really be anything that opposes God's input and guidance. Examples of some strongholds are given by Apostle Paul in Ephesians 4:25-32 like lying, stealing, corrupt communication, bitterness, wrath, anger, clamors, slander, and malice. Others may be unforgiveness, bitterness, grief, disappointment, addiction, depression, a negative self image, feelings of rejection, illicit sexual activity, and even activities in the occult. Some believe there are strongholds or spirits that hang over a certain region. Some believe there are spirits assigned to certain houses, to everything that belongs to us, to everything tied to us.

*****

Remember Jacob in the Bible? He was a swindler. His whole family had issues with this negative characteristic. His mom helped him plot to deceive his brother so she was a swindler too. And Jacob also had an uncle who was a swindler. Remember Laban? He tricked Jacob into waiting for seven years to get Rachel, but that was a trick. Swindling was in the blood. Not just Laban, but he had a dad named Isaac who lied and said his wife was his sister. Yet Isaac got his technique from Abraham who lied and said *his* wife was his sister. It was in the bloodline. It was generational.

In a sermon about strongholds, Brian Carn illustrates how there can be spirits in our households that we cannot get victory over such as one family divorce that repeats in later generations. That can be a type of spirit operating. There may be a spirit that does not allow success in business or one that can lead people to depression. Maybe there is a situation in which members in a family never reach their full potential. Maybe the women in a family constantly have relationships with abusive men. Maybe men have generations of family members of abandoning children.

We can ask the Holy Spirit to reveal that spirit operating in our lives that has caused the stronghold. Then we can pray that every stronghold that has come against us and our families would be completely destroyed. We will walk through such a prayer together at the conclusion of this chapter.

We can ask God to reveal situations in which every time something good is about to happen it falls through, or situations that cause us not to reach our promise.

Often times we may not actually be in the fire, and we are not in captivity in Egypt, but have not reached our promise either. We are in between where God wants to take us. We are in the middle and we are hurting. When we are hurting in the middle, we have to caution ourselves against certain tendencies that could cause us to develop strongholds.

Pain can rule our behavior when we are hurting if we are not careful. We often avoid boundaries in our lives and we make decisions that cause us to be mad at ourselves later. When we fail to be spirit led, we can develop a mentality of doing what we want when we want. It can also be difficult to control the things we say and do. But the spirit led person maintains a spirit of thankfulness and humility.

Focus on the blessings.

*****

When in the middle we need to make sure that we do not isolate ourselves or withdraw. Because we are in a pit we can get ourselves in another pit. Joyce Meyer recently spoke on these circumstances and said that God once told her she could be, "pitiful or powerful but you cannot be in both places at the same time. We cannot get from the pit to the palace feeling sorry for ourselves."

When we are in the middle we need to make sure that we do not believe a lie that God is punishing us for some former sin in our lives. Maybe there is some humiliating secret sin. Maybe it was an abortion 20 years ago. Maybe there is someone who believes they are being punished because you used to be a prostitute. As Joyce Meyer has said, that is nonsense. When God forgives us, the Bible says that He remembers our sins no more.

Stop remembering what God has forgotten. It can become a stronghold.

James MacDonald, Senior Pastor of Harvest Bible Chapel, taught six faulty views of God that can create strongholds. He identifies these views as common bad theology; God is a killjoy, God is a prison warden, God is a cranky boss, God is an absent father, God is a moody grandpa, and God is a scorekeeper. MacDonald argues against these views and counter attacks them using promises of God recorded for us in scripture.

God is not a killjoy. In Deuteronomy 30:19 we have this promise:

"19 This day I call the heavens and the earth as witnesses against you that I have set before you life and death, blessings and curses. Now choose life, so that you and your children may live." (NIV)

God is not a prison warden. In John 8:32 we have this promise:

"32 Then you will know the truth, and the truth will set you free." (NIV)

God is not a cranky boss. In Zephaniah 3:17 we have this promise:

"¹⁷ The LORD your God is with you, the Mighty Warrior who saves.

He will take great delight in you; in his love he will no longer rebuke you, but will rejoice over you with singing." (NIV)

God is not an absent father. In Romans 8: 32-39 we have this promise:

"³² He who did not spare his own Son, but gave him up for us all—how will he not also, along with him, graciously give us all things? ³³ Who will bring any charge against those whom God has chosen? It is God who justifies. ³⁴ Who then is the one who condemns? No one. Christ Jesus who died—more than that, who was raised to life—is at the right hand of God and is also interceding for us. ³⁵ Who shall separate us from the love of Christ? Shall trouble or hardship or persecution or famine or

nakedness or danger or sword? [36] As it is written:
"For your sake we face death all day long;
   we are considered as sheep to be slaughtered."
[37] No, in all these things we are more than conquerors through him who loved us. [38] For I am convinced that neither death nor life, neither angels nor demons, neither the present nor the future, nor any powers, [39] neither height nor depth, nor anything else in all creation, will be able to separate us from the love of God that is in Christ Jesus our Lord." (NIV)

God is not a moody grandpa. In Malachi 3:6 we have this promise:

"[6] "I the LORD do not change. So you, the descendants of Jacob, are not destroyed." (NIV)

And in Hebrews 13:8 we have this promise:

"[8] Jesus Christ is the same yesterday and today and forever." (NIV)

God is not a score keeper. In Micah 7:19 we have this promise: "¹⁹You will again have compassion on us; you will tread our sins underfoot and hurl all our iniquities into the depths of the sea." (NIV)

We need to make sure that we do not blame God for what has gone wrong. We can always trust God to give us the very best that He has in mind. God is the only one that can truly help us. We should not give up and think there is no way out.

Jesus said, "I am the way the truth and the life..." (John 14:6 NASB) We need to trust God and know He has a plan for us.

God does not do bad things but He can work good out of bad things if we trust Him for our victory!

When we are hurting we need to keep commitments. We should keep our word and do what we tell people we will do. We need to maintain integrity. People in society seem to have lost honor. We need to do right and be not weary in well doing.

Galatians 6:9 says, "Let us not become weary in doing good, for at the proper time we will reap a harvest if we do not give up." (NIV)

If there is something we cannot follow through with, we at least should have the decency to let the people know. Hang onto your integrity. It is in these times we build character. If we still do what God would have us do in these times we will develop more spiritually.

We do not get from the pit to the palace without going through the middle. We all have to go through the middle and how we handle it can determine how long it can take it to get there.

Anybody can do what is right when everything feels good, but when everything seems to be going wrong that is the time more than any other time we need to do what is right.

And in all circumstances we need to trust God. Psalm 91:2 says, "I will say of the LORD, "He is my refuge and my fortress, my God, in whom I trust" (NIV). The Bible says about Jesus when He was hanging on the cross recorded in 1 Peter 2:23, "...but kept entrusting Himself to Him who judges fairly." (AMP) I have both of these scriptures posted in my home where I can see them every day.

While trusting God, we need to make sure that we do not passively accept injustice. We must fight it! Fight it with what we know the devil hates.

Charles Swindoll said, "Life is 10% of what happens to me and 90% of how I react to it." When you are in the middle, do all of the good you can possibly do, for as many people you possibly can, as often as you possibly can. This is how we can defeat the devil. The only way to overcome evil is with good.

*****

God gave us dominion. God has made us leaders over the earth but some of us are fighting a limiting spirit. John Maxwell identifies this limiting spirit as the law of the lid in his book, *The 21 Irrefutable Laws of Leadership*. Picture a frog in a jar with a lid on it that consistently jumps and bumps its head on the lid. The frog soon learns to jump a little lower so its head does not hit the lid. If the lid is removed the frog will not notice. The frog will still jump the same level just below the opening where the lid used to be to protect its head from hitting the top. Some of us have hit our heads so much that we are afraid to break through the lid. But we must break through that lid to reach our full potential. But now we are going to pray and commit ourselves under the direction of the Holy Spirit to break through that lid. We must defeat those limiting spirits.

Maybe we have issues with making commitments. Maybe there are issues with starting something and not finishing. Maybe we seem to sabotage good opportunities that come our way. Maybe there are obstacles that consistently block us from getting to the next level. Could these events be revealing a stronghold or some limiting spirit?

What about other strongholds (or other kinds of spirits) that hold us in bondage? What about those that have been passed on from generation to generation? Think about families we have seen in which generations of men have had issues with uncontrollable anger.

As we think about our own lives, we should consider if there is something our parents suffered from that has now become an issue for us. Is it an irrational fear, addiction, or depression?

It can be almost anything but no matter what, God can free us from it.

My cousin and I were sitting at my kitchen table discussing how my dad turned out to be such a wonderful man and how different he was from his sibling (my cousin's mother.) My dad had such a terrible upbringing but was a loving, honest, hardworking, godly man, which was the way he raised his children, which was much different from that of his sister. She had a life that one thinks about when the term generational curse is mentioned. She and her husband were people always in crisis. They were married young as teenagers. They abused alcohol and drugs, and supported themselves with a dangerous criminal lifestyle. She had serious issues with depression, and attempted suicide more times than I can count. Over the years they had three different homes that were literally burned to the ground (at least one from arson.) They had eight children, the oldest of whom was accidentally shot in the head when his teenage friend aimed a gun at him and shot him, thinking it was not loaded. At age 16, my cousin was dead. Out of the eight children, at least five that I know of attempted suicide and two of the eight succeeded at ages 15 and 14. The remaining five survivors all have at least one child who has suffered from issues with substance abuse and depression. At least two of them have had children die in tragedy. One recently was an eight-month-old baby who drowned in a bathtub because her mother was taking drugs at the time and left the baby unattended.

When will all of this stop in this family? This was a beautiful family the enemy sought to destroy using strongholds. But it is not too late for those who remain. The strongholds can be removed and God can deliver. We plead the blood of Jesus over them right now!

When we begin to pray to remove the strongholds, God will do so. He will connect us with the right people so that these limiting spirits and strongholds can be lifted.

We can be in agreement right now that every stronghold with a limiting spirit operating in our lives is being broken! We must release it. Break it. Cancel it. Destroy it. Break it off of our lives. As we seek God, He will begin to give us direction, and at that time we must obey. Yes, there is work involved in spiritual warfare, but it is worth it!

*****

James MacDonald identified his personal stronghold as what he knew was evil music of the 70s. He would listen to hundreds of hours of this music and at this youth rally the stronghold was revealed to him. He said it took radical obedience for him because of his struggle. He knew he was stuck in a place where he was in the flesh more than he was in the spirit, more worldly than godly, more the old person than the new person so he rid himself of all of it. He would not even listen to any secular music until 30 years later when he was no longer in danger of it becoming a stronghold.

In his teaching on strongholds, MacDonald argues we should remove the stronghold supports in our lives, reconcile our view of God with reality (based on good theology), raise reminders to think differently, and review your identity and calling in the Lord.

We need to put things in our lives that will help us remember we have removed that stronghold and we have changed. Perhaps it will be a picture or an image posted as a reminder. And we need to put something of God in the place of the stronghold to replace the void.

Let's do something that helps us release the past. Think about what God has for us now. We can change faulty views of God and of ourselves.

My Uncle Phillip had a terrible motorcycle accident that crushed his ankle. The limb was initially repaired through surgery. Some of the bones were put together with pins and screws, but the pain did not subside and he was not able to move his ankle normally. After a decade of dealing with this impediment, his physicians told him his two options were to take pain medicine that would leave him like a zombie, or he could have the ankle removed. My uncle chose to have it amputated because his understanding was that removing it would include being rid of the pain.

What the doctors did not tell him was that the pain would remain; only he would have no foot. The phenomenon is known as phantom pain.

Phantom pain is pain that feels like it is coming from a body part that is no longer there. Doctors once believed this post-amputation phenomenon was a psychological problem, but experts now recognize that these real sensations originate in the spinal cord and brain. So my uncle is certainly not imagining the discomfort. Even though he has no foot, he can still feel the cold in his foot, an itch he needs to scratch, and the pain in the foot that is no longer there. Over a period of a year he still has not been able to get the correct prosthetic so that he can walk without a wheelchair or crutches.

Sometimes healing is a process, and it can be a long one. Sometimes God heals and restores in an instant and sometimes it involves a long time. How and when we are healed is up to God but deciding to be healed is up to us.

We must remember, with God, the recovery can be swift- even overnight. The spirit of God can do more in a second than we can do in a lifetime.

We do have an enemy lurking around waiting to erect a stronghold in our lives and the lives of our loved ones. In the movie War Room there is a scene where Elizabeth, the character played by Priscilla Shirer, is in her prayer closet or her war room, and she receives a download of the Word from the Holy Spirit and she begins to repeat over and over again "Resist him and he will flee." (James 4:7) The Word provides direction on how to deal with the enemy in 1 Peter 5:8 saying, "Be sober, be vigilant; because your adversary the devil walks about like a roaring lion, seeking whom he may devour" (NKJV).

Let's pray together using this prayer written by Stormie Omartian from an article in Charisma Magazine entitled *Warning signs you need to break ungoldly strongholds in your children.* This prayer can be used to break strongholds on our lives or on the lives of others. Just put the name of the person, your child, spouse, friend or anyone you would like. And modify it any way the Holy Spirit leads.

Lord, Thank You that You have promised in Your Word to deliver us when we cry out to You. I come to You on behalf of (name) and ask that You would deliver him (her) from any ungodliness that may be threatening to become a stronghold in his (her) life. Even though I don't know what he (she) needs to be set free from, You do. I pray in the name of Jesus that You will work deliverance in his (her) life wherever it is needed. I know that although "we walk in the flesh, we do not war according to the flesh. For the weapons of our warfare are not carnal but mighty in God for pulling down strongholds, casting down arguments and every high thing that exalts itself against the knowledge of God..." (2 Corinthians 10:3–5; NKJV).

Give me wisdom and revelation regarding him (her). I know there are areas of enemy operation which I cannot see, so I depend on You, Lord, to reveal these to me as I need to know them. Speak to my heart. Show me how to pray when there is something deep in my spirit that is unsettled, disturbed, or troubled about him (her). Show me anything that I am not seeing, and let all that is hidden come to light. If there is any action I need to take, I depend on You to show me.

Lord, I put (name) in Your hands this day. Guide, protect, and convict him (her) when sin is trying to take root. Strengthen him (her) in battle when Satan attempts to gain a foothold in his (her) heart. Make him (her) sensitive to enemy encroachment, and may he (she) run to You to be his (her) stronghold and refuge in times of trouble. May the cry of his (her) heart be, "...Cleanse me from secret faults" (Psalms 19:12; NKJV). According to Your Word I say that the Lord will deliver him (her) from every evil work and preserve him (her) for His heavenly kingdom (2 Timothy 4:18).

Let us again declare our Overcomer's Creed:

> I will get through this because God is with me.
>
> My walk through fire may be painful,
>
> And it may be long,
>
> But with God's help I will overcome.
>
> In the meantime, I will be wise and hopeful because
>
> God will use IT for good.

*For more study on divine revelation and to why bad things happen see the *Walking Through Fire* Bible Study Series.

THIRTEEN

Prayer Strategies in the Fire

In my walk through fire there is one thing that I have come to understand, if I do not spend time thanking, praising, and worshiping God, then nothing in my life works properly, and I do not have the proper resources needed to walk in victory.

- Dr. Lisa

Most of the time spiritually mature people can praise God and maintain a strong prayer life in the midst of any circumstance, but in the worst parts of my walk through fire I could not do it.

I went down so deeply I almost did not make it out. Many days I stayed in bed. I did not want to wake up because I was having a much better time being asleep. My life had become a reverse nightmare.

Generally, when we have nightmares we are relieved when we wake up, but every day I awoke to days of terror. I was desperate to end the pain, and sleep was the only thing that gave me relief.

David Foster Wallace best describes the kind of fear that had gripped me and turned into deep depression. He says, "…The person in whom its invisible agony reaches a certain unendurable level will kill herself the same way a trapped person will eventually jump from the window of a burning high-rise. Make no mistake about people who leap from burning windows. Their terror of falling from a great height is still just as great as it would be for you or me standing speculatively at the same window just checking out the view; i.e., the fear of falling remains a constant. The variable here is the other terror, the fire's flames: when the flames get close enough, falling to death becomes the slightly less terrible of two terrors. It's not desiring the fall; it's terror of the flames. And yet nobody down on the sidewalk, looking up and yelling 'Don't!' and 'Hang on!' can understand the jump. Not really. You'd have to have personally been trapped and felt flames to really understand a terror way beyond falling."

Advice that you get from some church people when you experience any side effects from a walk through fire such as worry, anxiety, or fear, is to praise your way out.

Pray.

Fast.

Stay in the Word every day.

Even though that is the right advice, I was not strong enough to maintain doing these things consistently during this point of my fire walk.

*****

It was a warm summer day and the sunlight I had been deprived of for so long pounded on my skin. It was warm and soothing. I could feel nothing in my body but the warmth from the sun on my skin. My mind was in a fog. Numbness had set in even though I had made the choice not to medicate myself to relieve the pain.

My best friend Pam, a strong person of prayer, stayed with me for a time when I felt God had abandoned me. My thoughts about this became deep feelings of resentment toward God so I could not pray much anymore, but Pam did. She prayed for me, with me and over me.

On that summer day I was lying outside in shorts and a t-shirt in the lounge chair holding both Max and Gracie, one of my dogs and one of Pam's dogs, when Pam came outside, knelt down beside me, laid her hands on my forehead, and began to pray. Most of what she said I could not understand because the Holy Spirit had taken over and she prayed in a heavenly language. Tears ran down her face as she cried out to God on my behalf. It was then that I experienced the gift of intercession in action. Something lifted and broke, and it *was* a something. It was as if a 100-pound weight lifted instantly from my chest. At that moment, I gained strength to pray a little.

Even though we have comfort as children of God in being able to personally speak into the ears of Almighty God, the trauma we may face sometimes seems too great.

We may feel we are incapable of prayer. When this happens, we are not able to access the strongest arsenal we have against the attacks of the enemy. We know that the enemy's one goal is to steal, kill, and to destroy. He does that by either convincing other people to harm us or by working on our own minds and getting us to harm ourselves.

*****

When we cannot pray it could be a sign that we are not in a state of good mental health, which is common when walking through fire.

Mental health is something completely within everyone's grasp. Even though it is not something difficult to address, the world has made it seem difficult, but God has all the answers we need.

In my walk through fire, there is one thing that I have come to understand – if I do not spend time thanking, praising, and worshiping God, then nothing in my life works properly, and I do not have the proper resources needed to walk in victory.

What do we do when we find ourselves feeling so weary that we feel we cannot pray?

What do we do when we have searched high and low for help and cannot get relief?

When we feel overwhelmed with life's challenges and we cannot do anything effectively, and we are not even strong enough to pray, outside intervention is needed.

In the fire we often experience toxic thinking as a byproduct of the pain we encounter.

This must be addressed so the enemy is not able to defeat us. Dr. Caroline Leaf has sage advice on these matters in her book, *Switch on Your Brain,* and in the electronic *21 Day Detox* program. Leaf suggests taking three basic steps that involves thanksgiving, praise, and worship to get our minds focused on God and our ability to handle situations effectively. I will explain the basis of it along with the imagery in a nutshell without venturing into the brain science behind its effectiveness.

When we thank God, He listens. When we praise God, we feel His physical presence. When we worship God, He works on our behalf. We need to keep God as our first priority. It is an essential part of getting a breakthrough so that we can have a more effective prayer life and get the forward leaps we need in life.

When we do each of these steps, Leaf suggests specific visualization techniques while we engage in prayer.

In taking a moment for thanksgiving, we can remember that the first thing God wants us to do is thank Him. We need to ask God prayerfully what He wants us to work on. To remember this, we hold our hands out and cup them and imagine that we are holding the toxic issue we are trying to get rid of. We need to close our eyes and asked the Holy Spirit to show us the first toxic thought or issue we need to work on. The Holy Spirit will tell us and bring to our awareness what He wants us to work on. Let us visualize ourselves kneeling down at the throne of grace. Once we have that vision, we start the thanking process and simply say, "Lord I thank You," then continue down the five-sentence gratitude list for about 10 seconds. Here are a few examples to use, but of course we can express whatever we want:

Thank You Lord for being with me.

Thank You for dying on the cross for me.

Thank You for the fact that I can bring all of my issues to You.

I thank You that despite this situation You love me.

Thank You for walking with me through everything.

Leaf explains that we are not thanking God for the toxic issue, but rather that He knows the way through it. Next, we drop that toxic issue we are imagining in our cupped hands on the floor as a symbol of casting our cares upon the Lord. It is no longer on us, nor in us. We must let it lie where it lands.

Let us take a few moments to do that.

Now you are going to praise God, which is deeper than thanksgiving. When we do this we can feel His physical presence. That is the promise He gives us. He inhabits the praises of His people.

We are not praising Him for the toxic issue. We are praising Him because He is with us addressing the toxic issue. Now we are still very specifically focused on *IT*. We are not jumping around to different issues, but are focused and disciplined on the specific issue. God will show us what to say.

The second step is to clasp our hands together and imagine that Jesus is holding them.

We then repeat our five sentences beginning with "Lord, I praise You" in place of "I thank You."

The more detailed we can be, the more specific, the more we can actually achieve mental health regarding our issue. Next, we squeeze our hands tight. Let us do that now.

Lord, I praise You.

I praise You that you're standing by me in this issue.

I praise You that nothing is too big for You to solve.

I praise You for caring about all my needs.

I praise You for protecting me.

When we thank God, He listens. When we praise God, He is right by our side. When we worship God, He acts on our behalf.

So now we are going to step into the deepest part of us, which is worship. Even if we may feel awkward, we are going to worship God by raising our hands. The posture of doing so is an act of submission to God. 1 Timothy 2:8 says, "Therefore I want the men in every place to pray, lifting up holy hands, without wrath and dissension." (NASB)

Worship Him.

Focus on God.

We do not think of ourselves; we just think of God. For 10 seconds we just completely focus on God.

Lord, I bless You.

You are an awesome God.

You are righteous and holy Lord.

You are worthy, Lord.

I love You, Lord.

We need to worship regularly to build up our ability to pray and lay our cares before

God. We can go through this process really fast or for longer periods of time, and we can do the three steps multiple times a day.

These basic practical steps helped me to be able to handle situations far more effectively than previously. I also met regularly with others to pray. However, in my walk through fire, I had to be diligent because it was common for me to feel like I was taking three steps forward and two steps back.

Often I felt I was toiling without progress, but I knew it was essential not to quit the personal disciplines I knew were important. I knew it was important to pray, read my Bible, gather in prayer with other believers, attend church every time possible, and keep myself engrossed in the Word.

I used this process to build powerful, strategic prayer strategies in hopes of becoming more spiritually mature. Soon, I was able to develop a much stronger prayer life and did not allow the circumstances to interfere with my relationship with God.

*****

Prayer is personal and unique to each individual. Even though there is much freedom involved, God provides powerful resources to help us pray strategically and specifically.

The most powerful prayer strategy to use is the Word of God.

Using the very words that God has already spoken is the first and most comprehensive guide.

As we seek God, He will guide us whether we are reading, studying, or meditating on the Word. The Holy Spirit will cause Scripture to be implanted in our hearts. Jesus tells us to "abide" in Him and let His words "abide" in us. These are the conditions through which we can "ask whatever you wish, and it will be done for you" (John 15:7).

Paul said, when we take up "the sword of the Spirit, which is the Word of God," putting on our spiritual armor, we can use the Word to "pray at all times in the spirit" (Ephesians 6:17-18), communicating with the Lord based on His living communication, the Bible, with us.

The Word can guide our prayers of adoration, prayers of confession, prayers of thanksgiving, and prayers of supplication, but certainly it is essential to use the Word of God in our prayers to battle the different levels of intensity of our walk through fire.

There are many different prayer strategies we begin to learn as we become spiritually mature.

Defensive prayer is knowing how to pray against evil.

Dangers do lurk with the enemy's many different arrows of attack and we must be ready. God's Word says spiritual war is taking place around us.

We must take up "the shield of faith so you will be able to extinguish all the flaming arrows of the evil one." We should trust and utilize the appropriate verse that addresses the specific temptation, deception, or attack at hand.

Priscilla Shirer actually polled a large group to discover 10 common strategies the enemy takes against us. He most commonly comes against our passion, focus, identity, family, past, fears, purity, hurts and relationships.

In *Fervent,* Shirer states we should make no mistake, the enemy will seek to discourage you from praying. He will "dissuade you. Disarm you by putting distaste for prayer in your mouth. He wants to see you passionless, powerless, and prayerless. Quiet. And because prayer is the divinely ordained mechanism that leads you into the heart and the power and victory of Christ, He knows you'll remain defeated and undone without it. Tired and overwhelmed. Inching forward but mostly backward. Trying to figure out why the hope an enthusiasm you feel in church doesn't follow you into the four walls you live within."

To combat the strategies the enemy has against us, Shirer demonstrates how to use the Word of God to pray His promises over our lives. For example, to combat the enemy's strategy to steal our passion, for guidance we can use scriptures like Ephesians 6:10-20:

[10] Finally, be strong in the Lord and in his mighty power. [11] Put on the full armor of God, so that you can take your stand against the devil's schemes. [12] For our struggle is not against flesh and blood, but against the rulers, against the authorities, against the powers of this dark world and against the spiritual forces of evil in the heavenly realms. [13] Therefore put on the full armor of God, so that when the day of evil comes, you may be able to stand your ground, and after you have done everything, to stand. [14] Stand firm then, with the belt of truth buckled around your waist, with the breastplate of righteousness in place, [15] and with your feet fitted with the readiness that comes from

the gospel of peace. [16] In addition to all this, take up the shield of faith, with which you can extinguish all the flaming arrows of the evil one. [17] Take the helmet of salvation and the sword of the Spirit, which is the word of God. [18] And pray in the Spirit on all occasions with all kinds of prayers and requests. With this in mind, be alert and always keep on praying for all the Lord's people. [19] Pray also for me, that whenever I speak, words may be given me so that I will fearlessly make known the mystery of the gospel, [20] for which I am an ambassador in chains. Pray that I may declare it fearlessly, as I should. (NIV)

These scriptures show us how the enemy seeks to dim the desire for prayer, dull our interest in spiritual things, and downplay the potency of the most strategic weapons.

Preemptive prayer is a protection and prevention type of prayer. Once we have experienced various attacks, we can understand the serious need to develop preemptive prayer strategies.

Proverbs 22:3 says, "A prudent man foresees evil and hides himself, but the simple pass on and are punished" (NKJV). Solomon tells us here the importance of having preemptive prayer strategies. We must learn to pray ahead of time about the events in our lives, commitments, and potential opportunities to the Lord. Spiritually fastening our armor and asking God to guide, provide, empower, and protect us before stepping into the heat of combat. The enemy's playbook and patterns have been the same throughout all time. If we know his moves, we can prepare and pray more specifically beforehand. He has signature schemes which include distraction, deception, division, or derision. Peter said, [8] Be alert and of sober mind. Your enemy the devil prowls around like a roaring lion looking for someone to devour. [9] Resist him, standing firm in the faith, because you know that the family of believers throughout the world is undergoing the same kind of sufferings." (1 Peter 5:8-9, NIV)

Extraordinary prayer is needed for the most desperate situations. Psalm 77:2 says, "In the day of my trouble I [desperately] sought the Lord; In the night my hand was [a]stretched out [in prayer] without weariness; My soul refused to be comforted." (AMP)

Extraordinary prayer strategies are those that go to the next level when situations reach a point of desperation like having a seriously ill child, a foreclosure notice, or the infidelity of the spouse. These unexpected moments of intensity call for radical, drop everything prayer.

We constantly see David using this type of prayer. In 1 Samuel 30, the Amalekites had destroyed everything by burning it with fire and had taken their wives and children captive. David was in great distress not only because of what had happened but also because the people blamed David and were trying to kill him.

When circumstances were critical, David sought the Lord first and never tries to do things on his own. He knew God called people to be a part of a body. One of his psalms says, "God sets the solitary in families..." (Psalm 68:6, NIV.)

One of the enemy's main tactics is to isolate us and to make us think we do not need others. David did not pretend to have all of the answers. He went to the proper man with the proper anointing (Abiathar, the priest) and pursued an answer with him. God answered David and told him to pursue, overtake, and recover all. And David did.

It is vitally important that we remain connected to a church full of prayer warriors who know how to break every yoke of bondage. It is important that we go where people know their gifts in the kingdom and are not afraid to use them. Together we can pray those extraordinary prayers so that we can be delivered from the strongholds in our lives.

At least 10 different prayer strategies are explored in the book, *The Battle Plan for Prayer: From Basic Training to Targeted Strategies,* by Stephen and Alex Kendrick. In situations in which we are walking through fire, we need to definitely know Defensive prayer, preemptive prayer, and extraordinary prayers, which are all essentially praying against the gates of Hell. We know this is very necessary, but as the Kendrick brothers say, we also want to be praying offensively.

We use offensive prayer strategies when we want heaven on earth. We want God's kingdom to expand and His will to be done. Only part of this task involves stopping the enemy and standing firm in the evil day. We need to ask God to open doors for the Gospel, to send forth laborers in the harvest field, to pour out His Holy Spirit in revival, to fill us with His love and the knowledge of His will, to use our spiritual gifts in His service, and to raise up a generation who will honor His name.

Spiritual warfare is about standing our ground against the enemy and taking new ground for the kingdom. Scripture says in Romans 12:21, "Do not be overcome by evil, but overcome evil with good." (AMP)

In our process to recover all that has been lost as David did, we can become an encouragement to others and begin praying for their areas of need. David was prophesied to be king over Israel, yet he had lost his family and was living as an outcast in the land of the Philistines. Instead of passing right by the Egyptian in need, David took a moment to encourage him (1 Samuel 30:12.) Little did he know that by taking time to help someone else, his whole life would change within 72 hours. At the end of three days' time, he would become king of Israel, get his family back, and receive forty years of plunder back from the Amalekites.

When we feel like giving up the most, and when things seem their worst, this is usually a sign that we are getting close to breaking through. Keep praying!

This time let's do the Overcomer's Creed with gusto:

> I will get through this because God is with me.
>
> My walk through fire may be painful,
>
> And it may be long,
>
> But with God's help I will overcome.
>
> In the meantime, I will be wise and hopeful because
>
> God will use *IT* for good.

*For more study on prayer, spiritual warfare, and spiritual gifts see the *Walking Through Fire* Bible Study Series.

FOURTEEN

Power in the Process

As children of God, when the Lord allows us to lose something, we have to have in our minds, in our hearts, and in our spirits that if God allowed us that loss, He is going replace it with something better in our lives.

– Dr. Lisa

Many, many times we experience attacks in our spiritual lives through no fault of our own. Simply nothing can be done about them. No matter what, seasons of distress may come and go repeatedly.

God has given us specific information in the Bible for a reason. He carefully selected which people and events He wanted us to know about and with overwhelming detail. What we notice is that all of us have endured seasons of attack and we have all had our own walks through fire.

Now, we as Christians understand that we have been given authority over the enemy and can easily respond to the attacks. We can rebuke the enemy, for instance when the attacks are on our health. We can say, "Wait a minute! My body belongs to God." When our families are attacked, we can say, "My family belongs to God and my house belongs to God. I command you, Satan, in the name of Jesus, take up your weapons and flee, for the Lord has given me authority." We can demand peace in the name of Jesus. We can engage in all kinds of strategic prayer, for we must follow the examples God has set before us.

But what do we do when we have done all we know how to do, and we still are subject to attacks?

What do we do when we seem to be under a pruning and a cutting in our lives?

What do we do when there has been an injustice in our lives and we are certain the weapons formed against us have prospered?

What do we do when we have rebuked the devil, pleaded the blood, anointed ourselves with oil, yet the problem persists?

What do we do when God has ordered our steps, but today He has ordered us to walk through fire?

We may believe that just being in the will of God means we will not get into trouble, but that is simply not true. Jesus was in the will of God when He went to the cross. Job was in the will of God and his life was plundered by Satan. Job lost his children, his health, and everything he had. He experienced lack of sympathy from his friends and his faith was stretch beyond imagination. Job abstained from evil. In fact, he shunned evil altogether. Of Job, the Lord Himself said, *"Have you considered and reflected on My servant Job? For there is none like him on the earth, a blameless and upright man, one who fears God [with reverence] and abstains from and turns away from evil [because he honors God]"* (Job 1:8; AMP).

Personally, I now know that no matter how much we pray and no matter what we do, the seasons of fire will come. Trouble finds us. We are all going to go through something, some *IT* or series of *IT*s.

The truth of the matter is that whom the Lord loves, He chastens.

We go through seasons in life when, in our fire walks, some things will be burned off of us just like the ropes around the wrists of the three Hebrew boys.

Some things will be pruned.

Some things will be lost.

A few of our brothers and sisters in Christ may say, "These things do not happen. We need to just name what we want and claim it." But I am saying that we can pray ourselves into oblivion, but every now and then we are going to go through something.

Somebody is going to die.

Somebody is going to get sick.

Somebody is going to accuse us falsely.

Somebody is going to cause us harm.

Even if we are connected to God like a branch to a vine, even if we are productive and producing fruit, He still may cut back the fruits in our lives. John 15 does tell us that vines do not produce fruit all year long, for in some seasons we will not bear any.

As children of God, when the Lord allows us to lose something, we have to have in our minds, in our hearts, and in our spirits, that if God allowed us that loss, He is going to replace it with something better in our lives.

We have to know God is going to do something new for us.

That bears repeating. God is going to do something *new* for us.

Now, for God to do something new, the old things have to pass away. Again, for God to do something new, the old things have to pass away.

God promises to bring us into green pastures.

What is amazing about God is that He will talk to us about plenty when we lack.

He will talk to us about feeling good when we are feeling bad. He will talk to us about joy when our hearts are full of sorrow.

He will talk to us about overcoming sometimes when we are at the weakest point in our lives.

He provides us with a vision for the future when we have none.

And He knows the difference between process and purpose.

What we are going through now is a process.

We need to remember not to look at the process but to look at the purpose. The Bible says that Jesus did not enjoy the cross and despised the shame of the cross. But for the joy that was set before Him, He endured it.

Sometimes we simply have to endure. We must say to ourselves, "I may be here right now but I am not going to stay here." Jesus had to say, "I may be in a tomb right now but this is only a three day situation and I am coming out of it."

When we had gone through the fire, we have attempted to praise God, trust Him, and serve Him.

We have had to endure some setbacks.

We have been cutback by criticisms.

We have been ostracized.

But we faced it with the attitude conveyed by the words of Job, "Though He slay Me yet I will trust Him..." (Job 13:15; NKJV)

Better. Something is going to be better. We are going to have better purpose. Better power. Better wisdom. Better insight. Better self-control.

We are stronger, wiser, tougher, and more tenacious.

We are more relentless. We must think it was good for us to be afflicted because we would have never known the power of God.

We need to forget the things that are behind and reach to those that are before.

*****

When we read the 15th chapter of John, we can understand when God took a vine through a pruning process. If you ask an expert gardener how to grow a prize winning fruit or vegetable they express two key necessary actions. First, the growing area has to be free of all old stuff (weeds and debris) and second, you must prune the vine.

Are we growing a life that could win any divine prizes?

Paul told the believers of the first century the same thing expert gardeners today say, keep our eyes on the prize.

Do you not know that those who run in a race only one receives the prize?

Run the race in such a way that you may obtain the prize. Growing something that wins a prize takes weeding and pruning.

After listing the names of great men and women of extreme faith and admirable character, the writer of Hebrews, in chapter 12:1 says, "Therefore since we are surrounded by such a huge cloud of witnesses, let us throw off everything that hinders and the sin that so easily entangles. And let us run with perseverance the race marked out for us" (NIV).

It appears that running or growing well does take weeding; getting out old stuff that might have been good during its season but has now become a hindrance to the current work that God is up to in us. It is hard to let go and clear the old away and move on, but if we do not do it the old stuff will choke out God's new work in us.

The truth is the greatest hindrance to a new move of God is often our continual focus on the last move of God.

When we have been through cycles and seasons of turbulence, and we finally get through, we can come out blessed and still be afraid.

We can be out of trouble and be blessed, and still be worried.

T.D. Jakes says it is almost like a cloud hanging overhead, where we are just waiting to go through something else because we have been on a cycle of distress and peril. What the enemy has done is to create a pathology of turbulence in our lives, so much that we are no longer expecting blessings. Instead, we are now expecting trouble and waiting on the next thing to hit us.

Christians always preach about Joseph and everything that happened to him, but what we are not made to realize is that once Joseph became the prime minister of Egypt, he never went back through the fire.

We talk about the attack on Job's life and his defeat but we do not talk about how God brought Job out of the fire. In the end the devil's onslaught in Job's life brought about recompense of "twice as much as he had before...So the Lord blessed the latter end of Job more than his beginning" (Job 42:10,12). The captivity of Job was turned around, (Job 42:10.) Job never went through the fire again!

Some of the challenges that we have gone through in our lives will never happen to us again.

Never again!

When Miriam knew it was finally over that's what made her grab her tambourine and beat it to the glory of God. She saw Pharaoh go down in the Red Sea, and God told her the enemies she saw that day she would see no more! We can imagine the feeling of relief Miriam had.

Whatever enemies we had in the past we will never have to face again. We need to stop allowing the past to hinder the future.

Whatever we have faced in the fire, we will never have to see again.

God promises in John 15 when we go through the pruning process we should bring forth fruit. We need to cast down the fear that we are not going to be productive in life again. We are going to be fruitful again!

Essentially, this promise means that God says He will put an order of protection around our blessings, as Jakes describes. God promises He will keep us and keep all that pertains to us. This means that He is going to make provision for us. He is going to keep our minds straight.

God promises He will protect us and the fruit we bear even before it is ripe. We must remember He said, "I will not let your vine cast your figs before time." This means He is going to stop us from moving too fast, because if we cast our figs before its time, we will lose the harvest by moving too fast. God also promises to protect us from going too slowly. He will cause us to bring forth fruit, which will stay on the vine until fully ripe, and then He is going to preserve His gifts.

God said we shall bring forth fruit and our fruit should remain. Nobody can take that away from us.

What God is saying is He will ultimately bring us to a place of stability.

God has called us to be stable, to be steadfast, to be unmoving, and to be always abounding in the work of the Lord.

For a moment, we can think about the process of suffering as a benefit.

We can think about the walk through fire as sort of a suffering graduation, and the honor given is transitioning from being a servant of God to that of a friend. We are becoming more spiritually mature. Jesus said, "Henceforth I call you no longer servants but friends" (John 15:15; KJV.) It may be that our relationship would not have been deepened with Christ without the process of suffering.

When Jesus can call us friends, He will no longer leave His will as a mystery in our lives. The difference between being a servant and being a friend is that a servant "knoweth not what his master does." Perhaps God allows us to go through trials that were unexplainable for this transition.

Is it possible we may have had to cry ourselves to sleep and go through unbearable trials to obtain this new level of blessing?

How do we know anybody can trust us as true friends?

We tell each other our secrets.

God is the same way. When we are friends of God He will tell us His secrets. Maybe not all of them, but He will tell us the ones He knows we can handle. When we fear, revere, respect, and honor the Lord, God *will* tell us His secrets.

He may reveal why we could not stay friends with certain people.

He may show us something great that came from our illnesses.

He will tell us our destiny, our legacy, and what He has in store for us because we have come to a place of stability.

He will show us that He dreams a bigger dream for our lives than we can dream ourselves.

We are going to receive the promises of God and we will bear much fruit, and this time nobody can touch it. In the Bible, the people of God had to fight the Canaanites, the Amalekites, the Jebusites, the Hittites, and so on. We have representatives of these enemies in our lives in the current day.

We have fought so long and hard that sometimes it is difficult to see and enjoy the blessings of God when we finally receive them. It is difficult to celebrate the victory when we finally walk in it.

But we must remember, when we walk in victory and finally come to the Promised Land, we must eat the grapes and enjoy the milk and honey, because God has brought us here for such times as these and we will never again walk through that fire!

Let's do it.

I will get through this because God is with me.

My walk through fire may be painful,

And it may be long,

But with God's help I will overcome.

In the meantime, I will be wise and hopeful because

God will use *IT* for good.

FIFTEEN

Release Reach Remain

Because this walk through fire may have hindered our abilities to release, reach, and remain in meaningful and lasting ways, we need to dig deep to build Christian based accountability systems around us to help us reach toward spiritual maturity.

-Dr. Lisa

For several months, I had nightmares of people chasing me, certain specific people. I would run to the point of exhaustion, for a long time, until I found a good hiding place. Or so I thought. People would pretend to be my friend and help me. But as soon as the perpetrators got near me, these pseudo-friends would nonchalantly point out my hiding place. The perpetrators would grab me, bind me, and come at me in my captivity with blunt objects to poke out my eyes, but I would eventually escape them. Though I am no dream interpreter, clearly the perpetrators were trying to steal my vision.

My nightmares finally ended on the day I wrote all of the elements of my *ITs* on paper and laid them before God, just like Hezekiah. I built a bon fire and I put them into the flames, releasing them completely to Him. At that time, I made a commitment to no longer allow *ITs* to hold me back. I would only allow good to come from them. It was then I began the process of reaching toward greater things.

I asked God to show me a new vision that I began writing down as described in Habakkuk 2:2-3: "² Then the LORD answered me and said, Write the vision And engrave it plainly on [clay] tablets So that the one who reads it will run. ³ "For the vision is yet for the appointed [future] time it hurries toward the goal [of fulfillment]; it will not fail. Even though it delays, wait [patiently] for it, Because it will certainly come; it will not delay. (AMP)

God promises that our vision will return. After I released everything to God, I went one step further this last year and traveled to Israel with my pastor, Tommy Bates, and a group of about 40 people. I have always been curious about the Western "Wailing" Wall in the Old City of Jerusalem. Given I was still in the middle of my walk through fire, I was especially anxious to get there. I was seeking any place where the power of God could possibly be present.

Built as a retaining structure on the western flank of the Temple Mount by King Herod two decades before Christ's birth, the wall has taken on tremendous significance in centuries since. Jews came here initially to lament the destruction of the temple by the Romans, but now the wall is a place of prayer. Pieces of paper with prayer requests are slipped between the cracks of the ancient stones. I had plans prior to the trip to write out detailed prayer requests of my own and to get everybody on the trip to do the same. We each had journals we had been writing in throughout the trip inspired by the verses in Habakkuk 2:2-3.

After traveling throughout the old city, we arrived at the Temple mount across the great courtyard and the wall stood illuminated, a fifteen-story relic of an ancient time. I was uncertain of the protocol because Orthodox Jews were bowing and praying rhythmically. I finally walked up and tucked my prayer requests deep in a crevice of the rock. I placed my forehead on the wall, and as my fingertips touched the stones and I began to pray, my friend Cleda began to pray over me too.

A tremendous peace swept over me and a sense of reassurance of the power of God came in both a whisper and a roar. Finally, I stepped back to notice the prayer requests in every nook and cranny, hundreds, maybe thousands. I thought about how long this wall had stood, taking on the many cares of the masses.

As we continued to walk the land that Jesus walked, I became even more acutely aware that the same power of God present with me as I prayed at the wall was with me everywhere I went. When I flew home from Israel back to New York I felt it. And when I got home to Kentucky I felt it still. What was different? Was it the Wailing Wall? Was it Israel? Was it spending 10 days with wonderful godly people having a good time?

It was perspective. I had released what was not in the will of God. I was reaching towards that which God had begun to show me in a renewed clear vision, and I made a decision to remain in them.

*****

Depending on the *IT* that has brought us to a place where we are walking through fire, we likely have lost our vision. Or perhaps it was taken. But God is a God of restoration and He *will* restore our vision. And God will restore many times over what the enemy has stolen.

What responsibility do we have to position ourselves so that God can restore our vision? First, we can maintain a strong prayer life, which is essential for a close walk with God. Second, we can be totally immersed in the Word of God. And third, we can begin to open ourselves up so that He can guide and direct us. When we go through something that causes us to be stuck to the point we feel paralyzed, we sometimes need help getting pulled out and set on the right path.

How can we get unstuck? What can pull us out of that place of paralysis and set us on the path God has destined? Yes, the enemy comes to steal, kill, and destroy, but Jesus has come so that we may have abundant life. So, what is our responsibility in receiving the abundant life that Jesus came to give us?

The process of the fire has changed us. Some areas of our life have been completely destroyed and some have been altered. Some have been formed just as God showed Jeremiah in the vision of the potter at the wheel, molding the clay. If we can think about our walk through fire again as we did at the start of our journey, let us think about that as we ponder what the fire has done to us on our walk. As we think about that, let us remember God's promise that everything works for good to them who love God and are called according to His purpose.

Let us fill in some blanks in our own thinking. As a professionally trained coach through the John Maxwell Group, please allow me to use some of the content provided by Christian Simpson from the Maxwell Team in the coaching training and certification process as we proceed thinking about vision.

Let me ask, what is our vision for the future?

First let us work on vision with this specific definition: Vision is a highly detailed mental picture of a preferable future.

Let us imagine life 10 years in the future. Whatever age we are presently, let us think about ourselves 10 years from now. Everything is different. Our life situations are 10 years different. Everyone we know is 10 years older. Our *ITs* are 10 years behind us.

Now why are we imagining this scenario? Because we need to visualize the hope that God has put within us.

Now let us pretend we are having a dialogue and we begin discussing how we have achieved everything we have wanted in life. We have become incredibly effective and God has blessed us mightily. We are happy and fulfilled and truly successful. We are fully grown trees with ripe fruit.

Let us name some of the accomplishments that we have achieved and even write them down. To achieve all of this success and to have the full blessing of God on our lives, we need to examine what decision we made exactly 10 years ago that got us off on this right foot. What decisions did we make that changed the direction of our lives?

Did we make the decision to delve deeper into our problems, or did we decide to receive deliverance and take the necessary steps to be freed from *IT*?

Did we make the decision to put off education, or fail as many classes as we could, or did we decide to pursue our self-development and give it our best efforts?

In our relationships, did we decide to hurt people or give the best of ourselves and add value to them?

Did we check out on life or did we plug-in to our greater purpose and begin the pursuit of it?

Remember now it is 10 years in the future and things have changed for us. We are no longer in the fire. We will never have to walk through that fire again!

Words mean things. The "best" words convey the right meaning. The less than best words may convey the wrong meaning or at least something unintended. For example, we should avoid using the term *lose weight.* While it may seem picky, think about it. What is the first thing you want to do when you lose something? Find it, right?

Now, I get that "losing weight" is generally a good thing. But a better term may be to "release weight." No, I am not trying to be New Agey, but is not the intent of the process of weight reduction releasing that which we do *not* wish to continue holding?

Imagine if our entire approach to life change was one of "release, reach and remain."

Release the things, actions, habits, intentions, and beliefs that bind us and keep us from achieving what matters.

Reach for the things, habits, intentions, relationships, and beliefs that are part of our change and growth.

We need to remain in full contact with them until we approach our goals. Then the process starts all over again.

So how do we release the weight? Well, we eat differently, we conduct physical activity differently, we think differently about nutrition, and so on.

How do we remain weighing less than before? By maintaining our new beliefs about nutrition, physical activity and lifestyle!

So imagine again then, 10 years ago, we did not "give up" something to gain the better thing – we released the things that did not help us in our goals and now we are reaching for the things that do.

Together let us remember to write our future history in a different way than our present trajectory by remembering who God is. With Him, nothing is impossible. Let us begin the process of what it takes to release, reach, and remain. Release that which we do not need and reach for those things that we do need. And of course, we may have no idea what the identity of either of these things might be, yet God will guide us. All of this will be part of the good that comes out of our walk through fire.

Every time we say this from now on, we will ask God to help us to release those things that we do not need, reach for the things that we do need, and remain in full contact with them if we receive the abundant life that God desires for us.

After we returned home from our trip to Israel, Pastor Tommy Bates shared that God gave him a prophetic word. Because we supported Israel, we would be blessed and we will have increase spiritually, financially, and influentially. This I will reach for and when received will remain in full contact.

*****

Because this walk through fire may have hindered our abilities to release, reach, and remain in meaningful and lasting ways, we need to dig deeply to build Christian based accountability systems around us to help us reach toward spiritual maturity. These support systems will essentially instruct and coach us through the process of healing step by step. When working through these issues we should not do it in isolation.

I have known of people who were instantly delivered from the anguish of life when experiencing a touch from God, but for most of us healing is a process. There are very specific steps involved in successfully releasing toxic issues and reaching for God's best for us. We need the help of the Holy Spirit in this process, and oftentimes we need experienced and spiritually mature believers.

Venting anger is an important part of the release. As we do this we will notice that the intensity of it will minimize and a variety of other emotions will take their course. This release is healthy as long as we do not allow the emotions to keep us stuck.

When we get to the point of feeling so stuck that we are not able to function, then that is where we need intervention.

We may need the help of intercessory prayer warriors.

We may need the help of Christian counselors.

We may need Christian life coaches who have experience with breaking unhealthy thinking patterns and walking us through the process of obtaining God's best for our lives.

Nothing can stop the destiny God has placed within us, although it is important to remember there are universal laws that govern the way we think and behave. However, these laws are God's laws, the universe just obeys. God is sovereign. He is in control.

Though the fire may at times be intense, remember we can trust in God's promise when He says, "Do not be afraid. For I have bought you and made you free. I have called you by name. You are Mine! When you pass through the waters, I will be with you. When you pass through the rivers, they will not flow over you. **When you** walk through the fire, you will not be burned. The fire will not destroy you", (Isaiah 43:1-2; NASB.)

Here we go.

   I will get through this because God is with me.

   My walk through fire may be painful,

   And it may be long,

   But with God's help I will overcome.

   In the meantime, I will be wise and hopeful because

   God will use *IT* for good.

*See drlisaministries.org for more coaching

SIXTEEN

Appointment with God

Some of the greatest miracles we may have are related to transformed hearts and minds.

- Dr. Lisa

Today we have an appointment with Almighty God.

We have it on our schedule for a set time and place. We can prepare right now with our list of specific needs to bring before Him. This is a good time to use your prayer journal if you have one. If not you can just grab some paper and start writing. Some people may want to record it using some form of technology.

First, we will answer these questions of ourselves and as the Holy Spirit brings the answers to our awareness, we will record them on our list.

Add questions the Holy Spirit may bring to your attention, but for now, this is the list of our opening questions what we will bring to our appointment with God:

What are some things that we are most stressed about that are stealing our peace, love, and joy?

What are our biggest needs right now that would take a miracle of God to resolve?

What provisions do we need from God which we and others would greatly benefit?

In what direction may God be leading us?

What needs of others in our lives has the Holy Spirit shown us that require God's intervention?

Take time to complete your list prayerfully, (even if you just take a moment to do it mentally initially), and then come back to this sentence.

*****

Now our lists are ready. It is that time.

We are prepared to enter the office of the Almighty God. It has been such an honor to share this journey with you. Keep these words with you as the journey continues, and please keep in touch with me to keep me posted on what God continues to do in your life. Whatever we may face, this is what we have come to know:

When we walk through fire, you will not be burned. The fire will not destroy us.

And...

God is able. He is able to do immeasurably more than we can ask or imagine. But the fact is that we know God *can* change our circumstances. Still, we do not know if He *will* change them. Yet, just because He *has not* does not mean He *will not.*

The bottom line is that God is able. And because He is *able,* and because He is *love,* our hearts are completely secure in every situation.

No matter how desperate.

No matter how chronic.

No matter how time sensitive.

Let's ask ourselves, what kind of vessel for God have we become as we have walked through fire?

Have we released the *ITs* that have left us disappointed, unsure, and confused?

If not, let us make our list and lay *IT* before God.

I do not want to limit the range of *ITs* or our walk through fire moments to outward appearances: family or relationship problems, medical test results, addictions, finances, legal problems, or loss. Let's ask the Holy Spirit to reveal all of it to us. Let's examine it all. Lord, reveal anything in our hearts and lives holding us back from your best.

Let us lay all of the *ITS* before God and then burn them (literally) as a symbol of permanent release.

Such an action represents that we are permanently laying our issues at the feet of Jesus. The paper with the documented *ITS* will soon be ashes. Yet very soon beauty will emerge and be evident in our lives. God promises beauty for ashes. We are about to experience miracles!

In this process think about the internal as well as the external. There are different kinds of miracles. Some are miracles we receive are for us. Some are through us. Some of the greatest miracles we may have are related to transformed hearts and minds.

Many supreme wonders have to do with obtaining peace in the midst of a walk through fire, as when God:

Refuels a lost passion.

Or refocuses an ignored, misplaced priority.

Or refreshes a spirit darkened by depression.

Or softens a heart grown cold and unforgiving.

Or exposes and transforms a negative line of thinking.

Or provides comfort during a time it is desperately needed.

Or introduces an amazing new friend.

It may not be, perhaps, as spectacular as getting the keys to a brand-new car or a big financial blessing. But these spiritual bounties are some of the most amazing work God does, and from all the attempts we have made to change our hearts over the years, we should know!

If it were so easy to conquer our stubborn streaks, or to calm our tempers, or ease our worries, we would surely have fixed them all by ourselves a long time ago.

When God surprises us by intervening in a way we did not imagine such as changing someone's mind, helping our spouse take a different attitude, reorienting our children's direction, softening our bosses' heart, bringing new godly relationships in our lives, or just brightening that no hope look in our eyes, we can be sure He has been up to something incredible, inconceivable, even borderline impossible.

That is because God *can*.

In her book, *God is Able,* Priscilla Shirer states, "I am more and more convinced that when we experience supernatural and extraordinary miracles that God performs in our lives, it is because He wants us to trust Him, believe Him, and expect Him. He does so because our primary goal is not for Him to answer our prayers exactly the way we have been hoping, but that we know Him more fully and intimately."

And when that change happens...

It is done.

I mean *really* done.

We know we can make it through fire in a once-and-for-all kind of way.

Whether we are in the fire or not, we must allow the comfort of God to envelop us.

Allow the Word of God to transform us.

Allow our wounds to heal.

And, finally, to make the commitment that regardless of the duration and intensity of our fire walk, we will be determined to glorify God in its midst.

Last time together.

> I will get through this because God is with me.
>
> My walk through fire may be painful,
>
> And it may be long,
>
> But with God's help I will overcome.
>
> In the meantime, I will be wise and hopeful because
>
> God will use IT for good.

*For more God's recompense see the *Walking Through Fire* Bible Study Series.

SEVENTEEN

The Invitation

Believe + receive = become

Simply believing is not enough. We must also receive. We must receive the free gift of forgiveness and eternal life to pay for all sins past, present and future. When we do this we become children of God.

- Dr. Lisa

If you do not yet believe, keep seeking. The Old and New Testaments both say that if you seek God yourself you will find Him. We also know God has a special plan and wants the best for our lives.

This is what God really wants us to know:

[11] For I know the plans I have for you," declares the LORD, "plans to prosper you and not to harm you, plans to give you hope and a future. [12] Then you

will call on me and come and pray to me, and I will listen to you. ¹³ You will seek me and find me when you seek me with all your heart. ¹⁴ I will be found by you," declares the LORD...

-Jeremiah 29:11-14, NIV

And

⁹ "So I say to you: Ask and it will be given to you; seek and you will find; knock and the door will be opened to you. ¹⁰ For everyone who asks receives; the one who seeks finds; and to the one who knocks, the door will be opened.

¹¹ "Which of you fathers, if your son asks for[a] a fish, will give him a snake instead? ¹² Or if he asks for an egg, will give him a scorpion? ¹³ If you then, though you are evil, know how to give good gifts to your children, how much more will your Father in heaven give the Holy Spirit to those who ask him!"

-Luke 11:9-13, NIV

You might believe, but you have never received. Your life has not changed. People have not seen a difference in you. God seems so distant from you. You may believe but there has never been a point in time where you have received Jesus Christ as your forgiver and your leader and, therefore, become as John 1:12 says, a child of God.

> ¹² Yet to all who did receive him, to those who believed in his name, he gave the right to become children of God— (John 1:12 NIV)

Let us extract the active verbs in this scripture: receive, believe, and become. Now let us put them in an equation and see what we find:

$$\text{Believe} + \text{receive} = \text{become}$$

Simply believing is not enough. We must also receive. We must receive the free gift of forgiveness and eternal life to pay for all sins past, present, and future. When we do this we become children of God.

You do not have to know everything to know something. With confidence you can know God exists and Jesus is His Son, and He is offering forgiveness and eternal life as a free gift of His grace. That's all you need to know right now.

Have you ever RECEIVED the free gift of Salvation?

If the answer is "No," do you want to take this step right now?

At the moment you do this you will become a child of God.

If you want to take that step then just say these words with a sincere heart and God will hear you:

Lord Jesus, it's true that I've fallen short of how you want me to live. I am truly sorry for that. Today, I acknowledge and I believe that You Lord Jesus are the one and only Son of God and right now, in an attitude of repentance and faith, I receive your free gift of forgiveness. Thank you for paying the penalty of sin in my life, so that I can have eternal life. Help me Lord Jesus to live the kind of life that you want me to live, because from this moment on, I am yours.

If you prayed that prayer, God heard you and according to John 1:12 *you* have become a child of God.

If you have made this decision I celebrate with you. This has been the best decision you have ever made in your life. Not only in this world as you build a relationship with the Lord Jesus Christ, but in the world to come.

I encourage you to do a couple of things: Join a local church that teaches the Bible, a place where you can grow and learn as a follower of Jesus Christ. If you want ideas on resources to go the next step visit the website at DRLISAMINISTRIES.ORG. There are all kinds of information and guidance there to help you get launched in the greatest adventure of life, being a follower of Jesus Christ. God Bless You!

STAY CONNECTED

DRLISAMINISTRIES.ORG

"The Lord has given me the tongue of the learned, that I should know how to speak a word in season to him who is weary..."
-Isaiah 50:4 a

Request Dr. Lisa

Speaking
Teaching
Coaching

www.facebook.com/drlisaministries

@ drlisahamm